MUSICAL
RETIREMENT

Enjoy Your Senior Years

IVGENI KRIGER

Co-authored with
RAYMOND AARON

Musical Retirement: Enjoy Your Senior Years

www.musicalretirement.com

References to internet websites (URLs) were accurate at the time of writing. Authors and the publishers are not responsible for URLs that may have expired or changed since the manuscript was prepared.

Limits of Liability and Disclaimer of Warranty

The author and publisher shall not be liable for your misuse of the enclosed material. This book is strictly for informational and educational purposes only.

Warning – Disclaimer

The purpose of this book is to educate and entertain. The author and/or publisher do not guarantee that anyone following these techniques, suggestions, tips, ideas, or strategies will become successful. The author and/or publisher shall have neither liability nor responsibility to anyone with respect to any

loss or damage caused, or alleged to be caused, directly or indirectly by the information contained in this book.

Medical Disclaimer

The medical or health information in this book is provided as an information resource only, and is not to be used or relied on for any diagnostic or treatment purposes. This information is not intended to be patient education, does not create any patient-physician relationship, and should not be used as a substitute for professional diagnosis and treatment.

Publisher
10-10-10 Publishing
Markham,
ON Canada

Printed in Canada and the United States of America

Dedication

For all the seniors in the world who deserve to be happy and feel good; retirement is the time that everyone dreams of reaching. I dedicate my book and work to giving instruments and tools to those working with seniors, so they can improve the daily life of seniors, bringing happiness to millions!

Table of Contents

Table of Contents

MUSICAL
RETIREMENT

Acknowledgments

I thank my grandmother, who confirmed to me that I should go with my passion. She supported me in following my dreams, and I am grateful for everything that she gave me.

I thank my parents, who endorsed my musical study and who later recommended that I should study nursing because they saw how much I love to help people.

MUSICAL
RETIREMENT

Foreword

Aging with music is this book's subject. If you run a retirement facility, how can you stand out from the competition? In Musical Retirement: Enjoy Your Senior Years, Ivgeni Kriger shares his journey to incorporating music into the lives of seniors. Along the way, you will learn how to incorporate music into all areas of your facility.

Ivgeni shares a typical day in his ideal retirement or care facility. It involves musical experiences throughout the day, from beginning to end. Along the way, you also learn how this perfect musical day can help you, your loved ones and your staff to connect with your residents in a way that will benefit them.

Next, Ivgeni shares his philosophy regarding mentoring for seniors using music. Throughout these pages, he gives you, your loved ones, and your staff tools to use in daily life that can be used for being guided by music. Each chapter is about music helping seniors find joy at their new stage of life and how to facilitate this idea.

Musical Retirement brings music into the daily

MUSICAL
RETIREMENT

routine, but also into those special times of their lives, such as birthday celebrations. Ivgeni also shares how you can incorporate various musical activities into the offerings of your facility, which can make it stand out.

If you are looking for an opportunity to speak to your current and potential residents in a different way, then Musical Retirement: Enjoy Your Senior Years is a fantastic guide to learning how to add music into all aspects of your facility's routine.

MUS CAL
RET REMENT

CHAPTER 1

The Ideal Experience for You and Your Aging Loved Ones

MUSICAL RETIREMENT

All of us will have to deal with the experience of aging and caring for an aging loved one. It involves making decisions relating to their care and finding the right environment to bring joy and fun into their lives throughout their retirement life. Perhaps you are dealing with a disease, such as dementia or Alzheimer's, which adds another level of care to the needs of your loved one.

Personally, how do you want to spend your retirement, and what quality of life do you want as you age? It is not just about finding a place with good medical care, but also about finding the best quality of life to compliment that care.

Clearly, there are many aspects to consider when it comes to finding the right facility for you or your loved ones. One of those key aspects to consider is their daily life and what activities are incorporated into it.

I want to share with you what I consider the ideal day for you or your loved one living in a residential care or retirement facility. Music is amazing; it speaks to the soul, to mental and physical wellbeing. Find out what makes my musical ideal day so different.

Let's start with how you wake up. Rather than a blaring alarm clock, wake up to music—warm tones that soothe the mind and compliment a restful night's sleep. In our musical residence, we help with getting ready to start the day by offering musical selections for them to enjoy. All of us have sung in the shower from time to time; for seniors, singing in the shower is a part of the daily routine, and encouraged.

Once ready to greet the day, our residents will enjoy musical selections throughout breakfast, allowing them to nourish their mind and body at the same time. Activities available for residents include exercises put to music, crafts, and so much more. Music is interwoven into all aspects of the day's events, from the first meal to the bedtime.

Music also can be a therapeutic tool, one that allows family or staff to find out what might be going on in the minds and hearts of those who live in my facility. Ask a resident to choose a piece of music. Your choice may reflect a positive and upbeat mood, but others may choose music to reflect their sadness or grief. In each case, music can be the tool to help the staff to reach out and open the lines of communication. This fights isolation for seniors, both physically and mentally.

Seniors may take advantage of the quiet and secluded areas throughout the facility, where you can be alone to meditate or relax, listening to music found on YouTube or through other technology mediums. You or your loved ones are taking charge of what you want to listen to, thus increasing your daily enjoyment and helping them to relieve their stress.

Classes focus on learning music, exploring the

musical history of a genre, or even learning to play an instrument. Carl Orff developed a musical method based on the pentatonic scale that permits easier access to performance for those who have not performed before. Activities with an emphasis on physical fitness or craft can still have a musical component, thus building the benefits of music into all areas of daily life. Our goal is to create an amazing and joyful quality of life, one that would make you or your loved ones excited to call it home.

As the day comes to an end, you would drift off to sleep listening to the simple tones of a light and peaceful musical piece. Your caretakers, each with a musical and medical/nursing background, can match music to your interests, thus individualizing your experience.

What is the Theme?

Throughout a musical ideal day, there is a constant focus on music in all its aspects. From the beginning of the day to the end, music connects you, your loved ones and the individuals who care for you. I bet that you are thinking to yourself, "That is how I would like to live!"

My mission was to create a residential care facility offering residents and their families an amazing quality of life through the gift of music. It is about finding ways to help you enjoy life, regardless of your physical and mental activity level. Throughout my career, I have not

MUSICAL
RETIREMENT

only had the privilege of caring for seniors at various points in their retirement, but I have also had the privilege of sharing my musical gifts with them through my saxophone.

What I have noticed is how much my musical activities in various residential homes have impacted those seniors who attended. I didn't just play a few songs for them. I also encouraged their participation, making it more than just another event to sit through. The point was to allow them to connect with another human through music. The results are often incredible, as I watch their faces light up. They enjoy the process, and it lifts them up. Their quality of life is positively impacted, at a time when they might be coming to grips with a loss of independence due to aging.

Today's residential nursing facilities often have to focus so much on the budget that activities which bring joy to seniors get a lower priority. I continue to work with residential facilities that would like to have me and my staff come more frequently, but it isn't in the budget. My experience with these homes opened my eyes to a real need in the senior community. It is not just about caring for their physical bodies. It is about their quality of life as well, serving them mentally and emotionally, as well as physically.

Nursing a physical body includes bathing, assisting them to eat, change, go to the restroom, take their medications, and so much more. The challenge that many retirement facilities face is how to keep their senior residents active and keep their quality of life high. To tackle these challenges, it meant creating a facility that was different from its inception.

When I focus on an ideal residential facility, I want to stress quality care for both body and spirit. My ideal day for seniors involves music because I recognize its healing powers and the ability of music to help us connect deeply with our emotions. Music can speak to us and allow our bodies to express thoughts and feelings through our movements. It is an unspoken language, but one that is so necessary for humans to experience.

For residential facilities, each and every part of the day focuses on both a resident's physical and mental wellbeing. Through music, I believe we reach that balance in a way that has never been achieved before.

Perhaps you are running a residential facility right now and want to incorporate these ideals and tools fully, thus positively impacting the quality of life of your residents. On the other hand, you could be a family member looking for the right residential facility for your loved one. Regardless of the circumstances, I want you to understand my vision of a musical residential facility and what impact that has on the residents' quality of life.

Along the way, I encourage you to take advantage of these tools to improve your quality of life now, regardless of whether you are in a retirement facility or still in the process of finding your new home. For seniors, using these musical techniques to incorporate music into your life can add to your quality of life. Many of these ideas bring music into your everyday life in a more substantial way. How did I end up incorporating my nursing career with music as a meaningful part of the lives of the seniors I care for?

My Journey to Connect the Musical with the Nursing

I was born and raised in Russia before moving to Israel when I was 18. My birthplace was a small town named Birobidzhan, which was built for Jewish people as part of Stalin's efforts to concentrate the Jews into one location. From childhood, I felt that music was a significant part of my body. My father played the saxophone, and I frequently watched him, enjoying the experience of listening and feeling the music. When I was 15 years old, I asked my grandmother if she would be alright if I left to go to study music. At that time, she was very sick, so it took courage for me to ask. My grandmother told me to go with my heart. If you go with your heart, then you will do the most for other people.

You have to love what you do. I appreciate her wisdom because it helped me to make choices that led me to the right path, which included studying at a musical college in Russia, before moving to Israel.

I immigrated to Israel as an adolescent. Russian aerial border didn't approve to take my saxophone to

Israel and I needed to leave the saxophone in airport in Moscow. It was very stressful. I cried there as if I was an infant. In Israel, God connected me with the educational Yemin Orde Youth Village. This village is located atop of Mount Carmel in northern Israel. It serves as a home, school, and safe haven for 500 at-risk and immigrant youth that come from around the world. The staff provides individualized care and academic tutoring, while weaving in the values of Judaism into every aspect of life. In Yemin Orde, I studied and later worked as Youth Guide. It was here that I met Chaim Peri, who served as an educator and director of this village for 30 years. Today, he serves as the Founder of Yemin Orde's Village Way Educational Initiatives. I met him after being in Israel for just a few weeks and he became my educational and spiritual father. Dr. Peri saw how important music was to my life and how bad I felt without my saxophone. He helped me to get a donated saxophone. Today, I still play that saxophone, using it around the world to bring happiness and fun to so many different people. Yemin Orde and Dr. Chaim Peri donated a lot educationally to my life!

I shared this story because of its significance to me. The experience was lifesaving for me and it showed how other people can feel our passion and help us. Our passion is our energy and our energy is our gas for daily life! Please demonstrate and use your passion every single moment. Dr. Chaim Peri taught me so much and gave me a living example that provided an inner impact

MUSICAL
RETIREMENT

to help people achieve their passion. I want to express a huge thank you to Dr. Chaim Peri and for Yemin Orde.

My time in Israel was where I realized that I wanted to heal people as well. I decided to study nursing. During this phase of my education, I saw that the way to cure and care for people has to be different. This was the period when I started to imagine my musical retirement home, a place where both mind and body would be cared for and seniors would be able to enjoy this next stage of their lives.

As part of my nursing studies, which also included mental health, I started to see how music could connect others and build a bridge of communication, regardless of their age. For many years, I worked in the mental health field, and I developed different musical groups with various objectives as part of that work.

In one of my groups, I would ask everyone to pick a song. You had to listen to the song choices of others, but they had to listen to your choice as well. After listening to the selection or a portion of it, I would ask them, "Why did you choose that music? How does this music make you feel?"

Individuals can find it scary to speak about their feelings, but in this setting, I create a safe space for them to do so. Now they can speak about their feelings and how their choice of song reflected them. Plus, others may have similar feelings, and a connection is created between these individuals. Friendships can begin, ones that allow for them to spend time together outside of the group.

My journey to creating a musically focused facility, and sharing it with you, truly began when I was in the nursing profession myself, particularly as I led these groups. I saw how much my patients benefited when music was added to their lives. I could see their eyes light up, and it was obvious that music contributed to their enjoyment of life, despite any challenges they were facing.

Today, I am the owner of Musical Retirement Corporation. My great staff and I work with senior groups in various facilities around the world, providing different and unique musical activities that add to their quality of life and keep them connected with others. Please review our website: musicalretirement.com.

The primary focus throughout this book is using music to make the most of your senior years by supporting your mental health. Depression and other issues can have an impact as we age, but music can be a way to connect with others and deal with those challenges in a positive way. The goal of my team is to offer seniors, both those living independently and those currently living in retirement homes, musical programs and techniques to fit your needs and provide encouragement and support to maintain your emotional and mental health.

For seniors, mental exercise is as important as physical exercise. Experts agree that there are few things that

MUSICAL
RETIREMENT

stimulate the brain the way that music can. Listening to music and unique activities related to music, can assist in reducing anxiety, blood pressure, and pain, as well as improve sleep quality, mood, mental alertness, and memory.

Our brains do a lot of work to understand the structure and relationship between notes. Even seniors who try to learn an instrument find themselves with improved memory and problem-solving abilities. The quality of life can be improved with music, especially for seniors who are entering a different phase of their lives.

Granted, I still had to handle caring for the physical needs of the seniors I worked with as a nursing professional, but I felt as if the music also allowed me to care for their mental and emotional needs as well as their physical ones. They could choose what soothed them or what reminded them of a treasured memory from the past, or a musical choice could be something that made them tap their toes and snap their fingers. It spoke to them on another level, and I saw the benefits firsthand.

When you can improve the memory and problem-solving abilities of seniors, you are helping them to stave off diseases that attack them mentally. Brain function can disappear without activities that encourage the brain to work and continue to make connections. The brain is a muscle that needs exercise, and music can be a way to exercise this unique muscle in your body.

Dementia is a disease that claims many of those who are aging, especially as it attacks the memory. Individuals lose their ability to stay connected in the present, and they also become disconnected from their past, unable to recognize loved ones or others. Music is a way to connect with these individuals because it can often help them to recall memories or emotions, thus enhancing their mental performance, especially after they have spent time singing classic hits or numbers from musicals.

Music also is a powerful way to evoke emotion, which connects us to our memories. I am sure that you can think of a memory that brings up a specific emotion, perhaps joy or sorrow. When music is paired with everyday activities, patients can begin to develop a rhythm to assist them with recalling their memories related to that activity. Another benefit is the improvement of their cognitive ability over time. Even if there is not a major improvement, the use of music can help stave off further deterioration, or slow down that process. I want to be clear that while music is not a cure-all, it can provide so many benefits throughout our lives and after retirement.

The reality is that as our brains degenerate, musical aptitude and appreciation are often the last two abilities to fall victim. Imagine being able to reach these individuals through music, allowing you to connect with the person, no matter what their mental state. These are just a few of the benefits for those dealing with these

MUSICAL
RETIREMENT

challenges, but the benefits of music for seniors do not end there.

The fact is that for seniors of any age, music can be a way to insert fun into their lives. Remember, part of aging is recognition of the reality that these seniors are withdrawing and losing interest in what they formerly enjoyed. Music, particularly singing, can be a way to help them continue to engage and keep their brains stimulated, and give them the opportunity to have fun, despite any physical and mental limitations. It also provides a way to facilitate cognitive function, and coordinate motor movements. Essentially, you are contributing to their quality of life by engaging them mentally and physically.

Part of dealing with dementia and Alzheimer's is the stress-induced agitation that can be difficult to manage. It can be difficult to connect with them because you are not always able to reach across the disease to connect with them. Music can be a tool to help you in doing so, allowing you to assist them in calming down by reducing their stress level.

Today, I continue to work in the mental and physical health fields while maintaining my connection to music. One of the things that I noticed during my time working in those fields is that I want to share happiness with seniors, giving them a better quality of life throughou their retirement. I show seniors that it is possible for them to do more, as part of my program involves them using their arms, legs, and voices. They can use their whole body, and since they are having fun, there is a lot of laughter involved as well.

It is an incredible feeling, to know that you have helped someone find the laughter and joy of life, especially if they are dealing with multiple chronic illnesses or chronic pain. There may be little that shifts them outside of the realm of their physical challenges, but music has that power.

The point of tying music to retirement and seniors is to help them continue to find fun and joy in their lives. Building music into everyday activities can do this in a way that doesn't have to be limited by chronic physical or mental conditions. Together, my staff and I focus on sharing musical benefits as part of their daily routine. However, it goes much deeper, as music can be a way to connect and discuss experiences from their lives and allow them to share their wisdom with others. Lyrics can be a way to discuss strength, courage, overcoming challenging circumstances, and even dealing with loss. As seniors age, the loss may be more frequent, creating a new challenge for them to address in maintaining their joy in life.

As a musician and a registered nurse, I understand the connection between the brain and the heart. Your brain helps you to translate the music notes, but it is in your heart where you make the true emotional connections with individuals. I want to convey that emotional connection throughout my work with seniors.

Music is also a great way to manage stress and

MUSICAL
RETIREMENT

moods. Part of aging, unfortunately, is losing the ability to do things for yourself. Independence is often difficult to let go of, making stress and bad moods a reality. After all, you can imagine how difficult it would be to give up your independence as a young person, so take those thoughts and put yourself in the place of an aging loved one. Music can become a bridge for the gap between the challenges of aging and finding the enjoyment of your life.

My goal is to help people who love music and continue to enjoy it, even if they weren't musicians themselves. The idea is that throughout every step of the day, the first question is, "What do you want to listen to now?" It becomes intertwined with their day, allowing for those cognitive and physical benefits outside of a specific class or activity. Even if you are a senior who is still at home, you can follow these tips and techniques to incorporate music into your routine. Here are just a few things that are part of our facility's procedures, starting with the caretakers themselves.

Those who are serving as caretakers in our facility have a musical background, allowing them to make suggestions to complement the tastes of the seniors they care for daily. Caretakers with a musical background should be allowed to play on their own instrument as part of the care plan for residents. In group settings, residents are developing interaction despite misconsensus. Musical committees made up of residents can create lists of music for the group activities, such as meals. Every three to six months, the seniors serving on the music committee can change, allowing everyone to have their voices heard regarding the musical selections. Activities throughout the day can also have a musical focus. For instance, imagine being able to take a class to learn more about music's history or a genre, or to learn to play a musical instrument or to focus on learning a specific composition. Throughout the process, connections between caregivers and seniors are built, which can be critical in uncovering needs that might not be as obvious to the naked eye, such as mental health challenges.

For musicians, this is an opportunity to express their love of music while doing their job every day. In this environment, your musical talents are celebrated, because they contribute to creating a fun and enjoyable musical environment for seniors. I want to move away from just having background music playing in the halls, to celebrating music in all of its amazing variations.

If you think that this type of care is what you and your loved ones need, then I invite you to read on and learn more about the benefits of music in a retirement home or care facility, and how it can positively benefit your loved ones as they age. The point is not to give up on them, but to keep them engaged despite the limitations that result from aging or chronic disease.

The premise isn't limited to just retirement homes or care facilities. It is about finding the enjoyment in this

MUSICAL
RETIREMENT

stage of their lives, just as they found in all the others. Taking charge of their enjoyment of life starts with shifting away from what they can't do and focusing on what they can do! Let me share how coaching can give them the ability to take charge of their retirement enjoyment.

The Ideal Experience for You and Your Aging Loved Ones

Please write down what are the most important things to you and your loved ones in a retirement facility?

_____

_____

_____

_____

_____

_____

_____

_____

_____

_____

_____

MUSICAL
RETIREMENT

MUS CAL
RET REMENT

CHAPTER 2

The Growth of Enjoyment Through Music

MUSICAL RETIREMENT

No matter who you are, it is important to take control of the enjoyment in your life. Seniors in their 60s, 70s, 80s, and 90s can develop the enjoyment of their lives throughout the day, from the morning until evening, and every moment in between.

While the first chapter of this book focused on creating the right environment for individuals to use music, the reality is that all that effort can be pointless unless you or your loved ones are willing to take responsibility for your quality of life.

If you want to be healthy, then you will take the steps necessary to be healthy. If you want to feel good, then you will do what is necessary to feel good. If you want to be happy, then you will do what makes you happy. Remember, you become what you choose to think about and focus on. If you think negative thoughts, then you will get negative results. If you focus on positive thoughts, then you will get positive results. You get whatever you choose to focus on. Just remember three words: **Believe and Enjoy!**

If you don't think about happiness, then happiness will not show up. Plant your happiness in your mind. It is the most important decision you will make in your entire life—deciding what you want in life. No one makes that decision for you because you are the one who determines what you think.

When you focus on happiness, then you will start attracting that into your life. To benefit from this, you truly need to understand how your conscious and subconscious mind works in relation to your body and physical world. You have to work on your self-image, the inner one. Every one of us has an image of ourselves. Let me help you or your loved ones with your self-image. I want to share a sample exercise to demonstrate how I work.

Please find your favorite song, or put on some meditation music, and sit down and let your body relax. Visualize in your mind how you would like to see yourself. Imagine how you would like to live your life. Now you have a picture in your mind, one that you can focus your conscious and subconscious on. An artist wrote, "I imagine my dreams and then I paint my dreams." Visualize your life with happiness and enjoyable connections with others, then take that picture and describe it on paper in the present tense. It makes a lot of sense because it helps to connect your vision with your thoughts. Keep reading what you wrote, and fix it in your mind, because **we become what we think about**. "Believe in your belief," said William James. Please remember a very important fact: **Our thoughts control our feelings, and our feelings control our actions**.

Family members, of the staff at any retirement home,

have an important role to play in helping seniors to reinforce their positive thinking and visualizations. Here is why doing so can be critical to their well-being.

Most seniors are losing the ability to do specific tasks independently. They may no longer be able to drive, dress, or manage their medications without assistance. Even handling their personal care, such as showering or using the restroom, may require help from others.

To gain a sense of independence, take responsibility for creating enjoyment in your life. The level of enjoyment in our lives is our responsibility until we die. No one can make you happy or joyful. Every human is responsible for creating a happy and joyful life.

One of the aspects that can help seniors reclaim their enjoyment is a coaching program with a focus on music. Through coaching, one is encouraged to develop self-responsibility in the area of enjoyment. My staff and I work with seniors and/or their loved ones, giving them the tools to build enjoyment into all their activities through our unique musical coaching program, but I encourage the use of coaches throughout your life for the unique personal growth opportunities that they can offer.

For seniors who are still living at home or with their loved ones, our coaching program is about helping them find enjoyment, not just when my staff or I are there, but even when we are not. For instance, a typical

MUSICAL
RETIREMENT

coaching session would include music and activities meant to help them destress or simply remain active. During the session, my staff and I will also focus on how everyone can do a modified version of this activity on their own.

Later, when we have left, everyone (family, staff, and other seniors) can remind them of those activities when they see individuals struggling or having an off day without any enjoyment. The point is to enjoy an activity. Building in those activities is a part of growing enjoyment in your life.

What is Part of My Coaching Session?

Many of the activities discussed throughout a coaching session involve focusing on bringing music into your life. Along the way, we want to give those we work with the tools necessary for enjoyment, regardless of your age. It is meant to help you reclaim the responsibility for enjoyment, not requiring others to be in charge of it.

Everyone needs help to develop that responsibility. Seniors could go to a musical coaching session once a month or more frequently as they feel the need. Below are some of the ways to build skills in seniors to create enjoyment in their lives on a daily, weekly, and monthly basis.

Answering the following questions during a coaching

session can help you to determine the areas where you or a loved one may need to focus attention.

How can I enjoy today?—This is the first question you should ask yourself every day. This question will help you to focus on creating enjoyment in your life by getting you in the right mindset before you even get out of bed.

Recognize that you might not know the answer to that question, but you can think about it for a few seconds. You might even jot down a few ideas on a piece of paper before you get out of bed. Keep that paper with you and refer to it throughout the day.

The point is to get your brain in motion. After a few hours, you are likely to start to see your creativity emerge and different ideas pop up. You are also going to be more likely to see opportunities throughout the day and during your interactions with others. You might also be more open to attending a musical or artistic event at your local library or college.

At the end of the day, after including music and the arts into your daily activities, it is important to ask yourself how you made the day enjoyable. Develop the skills to open your eyes and ask the right questions to create an enjoyable life. You need to ask yourself the right questions throughout the day, focusing on how to make

MUSICAL
RETIREMENT

your day enjoyable. In my coaching session, you or your loved ones will find the answers to your questions.

Another important question to ask is what kind of music you are in the mood to listen to right now. At the start of the day, your musical choice can help you to figure out the kind of mood you are in. If you wake up feeling in a good mood, you might choose a musical option that is upbeat and gets your toes tapping.

On the other hand, if you are in a bad mood or not feeling your best, then you might choose a musical selection reflecting that, perhaps with a deeper bass or a stronger beat. If you are feeling sad, that might be manifested in a slower musical piece, one that reflects that woeful feeling or your introspective mood related to some memory or loss.

The point is that no matter what you choose, it says something about your mood and the state of mind you are in. Once you have an idea of your mood or what is capturing your thoughts, then you would be able to choose activities that could help you lift your mood if necessary. Awareness is a very important step in your healing process. Through the right questions and music, you can quickly become aware of your feelings, and that awareness can allow you to act.

Part of the coaching process is about changing your mindset and making it part of your routine to think about your mood and the events of the day in the form of music. Often, music is referred to as a language, a way to express yourself and your feelings without necessarily using words. How can you use this musical language? Perhaps you might ask yourself what type of music would describe your day. You might feel in the mood for a specific artist or musical genre. However, if you are looking to change your mood, you might prefer to choose a musical artist that you associate with a joyful experience or an upbeat feeling.

At the end of the day, if you focus on bringing enjoyment into your day, then you are going to find that you are less likely to be tired or low on energy because you are focused on the positive instead of the negative. Music can help you to increase your creativity, as well as to describe your day to someone else.

When we enjoy ourselves, we draw others to us. However, there is another way to quiet your mind and allow you to focus on ways to bring joy into your life, and that is through your breathing.

Changing Your Breathing to Change Your Mindset

Supportive breathing is an important part of developing an enjoyable life. For example, when you ask yourself in the morning the question regarding how you can enjoy the day, you can employ supportive breathing. Doing so makes it a powerful way to focus your mind on finding enjoyment in your life.

MUSICAL
RETIREMENT

Combining multiple techniques can help you to keep your mind searching for joy, and it also helps you to cultivate the right mindset, one that you can share with others.

Here are five main therapeutic breathing techniques that can help you to do the type of relaxing breathing necessary for you to support your enjoyable life and contribute to the mindfulness you want to develop.

- **Equal breathing**—This type of breathing is meant to calm the nervous system, increasing your focus and reducing your stress. Inhale for four counts and then exhale for four counts, doing all of it through your nose. This type of breathing can be done in any situation and provides a simple way to calm your mind.

- **Abdominal breathing**—This breathing technique can help you to immediately reduce your heart rate and blood pressure, particularly during stressful times. Place one hand on your belly and one hand on your chest. Then take a deep breath, one that inflates your belly enough to stretch your lungs. Take six to ten deep and slow breaths during this exercise.

- **Alternative nostril breathing**—This exercise can help you to feel focused or energized, as well as bringing calmness and balance. Get into a comfortable or meditative pose, then hold your right thumb over the right nostril and inhale deeply through your left nostril. At the peak of your inhalation, block the left nostril and exhale through your now unblocked right nostril. Continue this pattern, shifting the inhaling nostril with each breath.

- **Progressive relaxation**—This process can be useful for reducing stress and tension in a work environment, at home, or even if you are traveling. Close your eyes and focus on tensing and relaxing each muscle group for just a few seconds each. Start with your feet and toes, before moving upward through your body, while maintaining slow and deep breaths. Start each breath with inhaling as your muscles tense, and then holding it for a count of five before breathing out through your mouth.

- **Supportive breathing**—I developed these techniques based on my research and professional experience. Start by inhaling in slowly through the nose, keeping the air in your lungs for 3 to 5 seconds. Inhale slowly and deeply, focusing on how the air is going deep into your lungs. The goal is that most of the air will go into your lungs and not into your chest. It is important to do this in order for supportive breathing to be effective. The result is that the

MUSICAL RETIREMENT

physiological process will happen even faster. Then very, very slowly let the air out of your mouth before drawing in the next breath through your nose. This is work for both your body and your mind. You may even feel tired and want to rest after completing one session of supportive breathing. Switch to regular breathing for a minute before continuing with the supportive breathing technique. When you master this technique, you will need just five or six supportive breaths to feel better. From my experience, supportive breathing is the most effective technique for cleansing our body and soul. The goal is to breathe slowly, allowing your mind and body to relax and connect with each other. Doing this type of breathing is important, both physically and mentally. Connect it with the music that you enjoy the most. We teach individuals to breathe in and out slowly to the beat of the music. As they do, then they are tying music and breathing to the enjoyment in their minds.

Therapeutic breathing helps you to physically release stress and a bad mood that might be brewing. Supportive breathing helps to connect your soul to your brain, and your brain to your soul, more effectively, allowing you to connect to another world—the world of relaxation, the world of hope, and the world where you know that all will be better. I call that a positive world.

As seniors age, the reality is that there are the losses of family and friends to deal with, and the grief related to those losses. Using breathing and music to release the sadness and grief can help to deal with those losses. Others might use it to help them deal with the sadness relating to the loss of independence as they age. Breathing exercises can be used in a variety of circumstances to provide mental quiet or physical relief from various emotions.

The point of a coaching program is to focus on how various musical choices, along with different breathing exercises and various questions can get the mind focused on creating enjoyment in all areas of life. For seniors, taking the responsibility for increasing their enjoyment can be done whether they live in a retirement home, care facility, or even with family members.

Shifting Your Environment to Grow Connections

Another part of the coaching process is to shift your environment, using activities such as taking mindful walks, hiking, or even sharing books or activities with a friend. These physical activities can also help you to clear your mind, allowing you to focus on other aspects of your life. For example, as you take a mindful walk, you can also be practicing meditation or even using that time to connect with God through prayer.

Individuals often find joy in building connections through simple acts of kindness, participating in community events, or finding ways to work with your spiritual worship center. All these things can continue to be a part of your life, even if you or your loved ones are facing physical limitations.

Perhaps you are looking for ways to build new friendships or connect with family members that you haven't seen in a while. In addition, you may be able to connect with a yoga class or walking club through either your local senior center or program manager in your facility. Take the time to visit a park, join a club, or play with an animal. Activities help you grow your connections—don't allow them to disappear just because you or your loved one is aging.

The focus of this journey is to help you remember that self-care is very important, even if you are not as independent as you used to be. If you are living at a facility, then working with the staff can be the key to helping you to implement your self-care plan, such as spiritual care services or a wellness center.

Ask yourself a few questions as you shape your self-care plan:

- What am I doing and where?

- What is my start date and end date for this activity?

- Who or what else could help me to reach my self-care goals?

These can be broken down by physical, emotional, cultural, social, and spiritual activities. Doing so can help you to create a short and long-term plan for your life.

Remember, our coaching is about teaching you how to harness these different tools and your musical choices to bring real joy and happiness into your life.

Please join our coaching program by contacting us today at musicalretirement.com. Part of this process involves understanding your musical journey, which is what I want to discuss next.

MUSICAL
RETIREMENT

MUS CAL
RET REMENT

CHAPTER 3

Your Musical Story

MUSICAL RETIREMENT

We all have a personal story, one based on our experiences and relationships, as well as what we gained from them. For someone who sees the benefits of music in everything, I believe that our lives can also be set to music. When a particular song comes on, it can often trigger a memory of a time in our lives where we were happy, joyful, sad, grieving, or angry. The power of music is undeniable, particularly because of how deeply it ties us to our emotions.

Part of this chapter is about exploring the music that tells the story of your life and how it can be used to impact your emotional well-being today. With that in mind, let's start by exploring the various phases of your life and how music ties into various events.

Growing Up Musically

No matter who you are, there is a musical group or a few songs that remind you of your childhood or teenage years. You might be reminded of specific individuals or events that shaped who you are and informed the person you are today. Additionally, there is a connection through music to our families and friends, as well as the context of when we grew up. Music can be the tie that connects you to your generation, those individuals who are contemporaries.

On social media, there are frequently posts that talk about experiences or individuals related to those who grew up in the 1970s, 1980s, or 1990s. Each of these posts appeal to individuals because it reminds them of a simpler time, and they can relate to those common experiences. Music has the same ability to remind us of various experiences and events in our lives, thus creating a commonality from one individual to another.

Part of my job as a musical coach is to think about and explore your life through music. Your personal musical history, your childhood, and even the music that spoke to you as a teenager, all of it plays a part in understanding who you are now. I prefer to use music from your past as a means to solve problems or challenges that you are dealing with right now. It can also be a way to manage your daily life, particularly the stress that comes with various physical challenges.

How Does this Amazing and Exciting Process Work?

First, I start by asking you questions regarding your childhood, focusing on various types of music. I want to dig down into your early experiences with music, particularly the music from your childhood. After all, your childhood memories serve as the base for many of your decisions, beliefs, and values. These questions might include:

- What type of music did you enjoy?

- What type of music got on your nerves?

- What is the first song that you remember?

- Share with me the various genres or types of music that you enjoyed or continue to enjoy.

- Is there a particular type of music that you associate with your parents or grandparents?

- Please share a few of your memories where music was involved.

Along the way, I may also ask about your culture and the musical influences that come from it. Many of us can relate music to a specific event related to coming of age. In the Jewish culture, for example, there are musical compositions, done through the voices of the congregation, associated with various religious events throughout the year.

Throughout this exploration, I will be listening to your stories, gathering information about who you are and how music impacted your life. For example, one individual might reflect with joy upon a song that her father used to play as they cleaned the house. She could share how much fun it was to dance and clean, making a chore into a game that got everyone involved.

MUSICAL
RETIREMENT

When she hears that song today, the fun and joy from her childhood comes bounding back, and it lifts her up emotionally. That same process can happen for you, and my goal is to give you the tools to do that successfully, especially during times of struggle, grief, or hardship.

The process begins with me taking a musical history, much the same way that they do a medical history when you begin treatment with a new doctor or have to go to the hospital for an emergency or scheduled procedure. Think about the doctor or nurse that sits down with you, asking various questions, learning about your past illnesses, your medications, your past surgeries, and other information that helps them to understand what you have been through physically.

One of the amazing things that I have seen as a result of taking this musical history from individuals is that you can immediately bring a smile to someone's face. I have interviewed 70 and 80-year-olds, who have all begun to smile thinking about the beginning of their lives and the music associated with that time period.

They start to remember songs and experiences from when they were five, ten, or fifteen years old. I find they can give me a song for every five years of their lives, and using that, I can help them to make connections with the songs of the past to address their problems today.

With our listening to that song together, which can easily be found on YouTube or another music outlet, I can help you draw some parallels in your life. After listening to a few minutes of the song, I help you to draw some connection, an association with the song, and what is happening now. I might also ask you about songs that make you feel happier or bring a sense of joy in your life.

These songs may also be played, and along with a few questions, I can help you to describe the best solution to your current situation. Now you have a connection to a happier time, and you are able to put that feeling to use in finding your solution to addressing your current issues.

Our bodies react when we listen to something, especially songs that bring us happiness and joy. Plus, we start to create some positive energy, and when you start to feel this energy, the right energy, then your brain starts to shift into a positive line of thinking. Once you start thinking positively, then you are going to be more powerful in all areas of your life.

I encourage you to spend time listening to music and using breathing exercises to help you bring clarity and focus into your mind. The point is to help you gain control over your thoughts and allow them to shape your feelings and actions.

One of the ways that you will be more powerful as a result of this process is that your brain will start to create solutions or ways to resolve your problem. By yourself, you create the solutions, simply because you created the right energy to feed your brain as part of the process. It is a shift, but one that can benefit you regardless of your age.

MUSICAL
RETIREMENT

When you think about the realm of psychology and working with a psychologist, it is not that they give you the answers to your problems. Instead, they ask question after question, prompting your brain to come up with the right solution to address your issue. In the end, you have everything that you need to be successful.

My staff and I work in the same way. I want you to come up with the solutions, and by helping you to create that positive energy through music, I am giving you the tools to create those solutions. Part of my process is understanding why certain songs trigger specific emotional responses.

Working with various individuals, I have found that once I have an understanding of your musical history, then I can really understand your life through your musical choices. When I listen to your songs, and you explain your connection to those musical choices, I can even suggest a variety of similar songs that can contribute to creating or building that positive energy in your life.

Understanding Your World Through Music

Throughout this process, I want you to realize that it is about connecting you with the joy and happiness that you have already experienced, allowing you to tap into that energy to address your current challenges. Aging brings several challenges that are not only physical, but mental and emotional as well.

However, you can still bring joy and happiness into your life, regardless of your circumstances. Aging cannot take away your joy, unless you choose to let it do so. It is something from my heart and understanding of people that allows me to use music to address a number of issues.

One of my many experiences relates to working with those dealing with depression. After all, seniors who feel isolated from their families and friends can easily slip into a depressed mental state. Those who suffer from severe depression just sit silently. There is no sound from them at all. They have expressed an unwillingness to talk. This is one sign of depression, but there are many others.

To those suffering from depression, you might be asking questions but receiving little to no response in return. My answer was to start trying to reach them through music. I would play 30 seconds to a minute of a song. They might not have wanted to listen at first, but gradually, I convinced them to listen, even if it was just for a few minutes. Bit by bit, I saw them start to open up as we listened to several songs together. They would start talking to me, speaking just a little, but enough to encourage me to keep trying.

It was about creating interactions, even small ones, which allow them to connect with another human being throughout their day. It is enough just to listen to

MUSICAL RETIREMENT

music with an individual and watch their expressions tell the story of how that song or music has impacted them. Connections, particularly as we age, are critical to happiness and enjoyment of your life.

As humans, we crave the touch of others, their company, and the ability to share what is in our hearts and minds. I believe that music is a critical tool for caretakers, to help them reach their elderly patients, even if they have gone silent. Within a musical retirement home, these connections grow with time and with the daily inclusion of music. Clearly, it can bring a lot of benefits when put into practice.

Those observations teach us a lot about the individual and what they might be dealing with in their lives. Along those lines, I want to specifically focus on how you can use music to address various stressful situations, particularly those related to seniors.

MUS|CAL
RET|REMENT

CHAPTER 4

The Benefits of Music

MUSICAL RETIREMENT

Part of my journey to the creation of a musically inspired retirement involved my growing knowledge of the benefits of music. Throughout my time working with individuals in the medical community, I recognized how important it is to engage individuals both mentally and physically in their care. Those that were engaged in activities, which were meant to help them stay positive and upbeat, often had better overall results.

The point was to build the right thinking and allow you to remain engaged in something outside of your current physical challenges. That positivity was the key to keeping your spirits up. For me, music was the key to helping those I worked with to stay engaged in their healing process. Music offers an option to help you deal with various challenges related to aging, as well as healing.

I have already mentioned how music can help bring back fond memories of the past, or how it can uplift someone's mood. However, there are more benefits, which can be critical to helping you or your older loved ones find enjoyment in their lives. People are born with the ability to tell the difference between music and noise. Our brains create different pathways to process the various parts of music, including pitch, melody, rhythm, and tempo.

There are also different physical reactions when it comes to different types of music. For instance, fast music can increase your heart rate, breathing, and blood pressure. On the other hand, slower music can actually have the opposite effect, providing a way to calm the body. Think of all the lullabies that babies and young children listen to as parents try to put them to sleep. Those softer tones allow the body to relax, making it easier for someone to fall asleep.

There are multiple effects on individuals, related to music. While all the impacts are not completely understood, studies continue to show that when you hear the music you like, your brain releases dopamine, a chemical in your body that can have a positive effect on your mood. Therefore, if you are looking to improve someone's mood, then music can be a means to do so.

Additionally, music taps into our emotions, allowing us to feel strong emotions, including sadness, joy, and even fear. Clearly, music has the power to move us and trigger our brains in either a positive or negative way. Researchers continue to discover the ways that music can impact us either physically or mentally.

The overarching goal of using music as part of therapy for seniors is meant to help achieve the objectives for the individual enjoying the music and its benefits. When I work with different facilities, my focus is about helping seniors find enjoyment in their lives through music. My events are part of a larger goal that gives seniors and their facilities the tools to bring these benefits into their lives, even when they are not able to enjoy one of my sessions.

Here are a few of the ways that music can be of benefit, making a living situation with music as the focus ideal.

Improving Your Mood

No matter who you are, there are days when you are in a bad mood. Specific events, such as the loss of a loved one, or just the trying circumstances that come with growing older, can negatively impact your mood. If you are also dealing with a chronic condition, then you may be dealing with various degrees of pain as well.

When I encourage the use of music as part of your morning routine, that focus is meant to benefit you by taking your attention away from your pain or other physical issues, thus improving your mood. With an improved mood, you are better equipped to enjoy your day, despite the challenges you might be facing.

Additionally, studies show that listening to music can benefit your overall well-being, including assisting in regulating your emotions. That can assist in creating happiness and relaxation in everyday life, regardless of the circumstances that you might be dealing with. For seniors, in particular, that type of benefit can be the key to maintaining the quality of their lives as they age.

Then there is the reality that depression can strike at any age but can be more challenging to manage as you age and feel more isolated. Music can be a way for my team and me to connect with seniors who might be struggling with this issue, and to address it before depression becomes too much and ends up swamping them mentally.

For seniors who are dealing with challenging circumstances, that uplift of their mood can be critical. The goal of using music throughout the day is to allow for those uplifting benefits to be applied consistently. Think of it as regular mood maintenance, which is what is beneficial at all ages.

Reducing Anxiety and Stress

Another key benefit of using music as part of your routine is that it can help to reduce anxiety and stress. After all, there is a mental stress that becomes part of our lives as we age. Independence is decreasing, and the things you used to do without thinking twice are now full of potential risks. Let's take the idea of getting dressed and ready in the morning. There is the risk of slips due to the reality that balance is compromised as you age. The bathroom is now full of obstacles that might not have existed just a few decades ago.

Can you imagine the mental stress this creates? Your criteria for risk assessment changes as you age, and it brings a different level of stress and worries into your life. Perhaps you have noticed that you or your senior loved one is more concerned with slipping, falling, or other safety options than they were in the past. When you start adding music into your or their daily routine, it can be a great way to relieve their stress level even as they deal with these challenges.

On top of that, there is a level of anxiety that comes with losing a beloved mate, family, and friends. After all, your social circle continues to get smaller as you age, and lifetime family and friends leave the scene. That doesn't mean you are unable to make new friends, but simply that your social life is changing. You might not be up to participating in old hobbies or activities, but together with that, you now have the opportunity for new hobbies or activities.

What I love about music is that it is timeless. You can enjoy music regardless of your age or physical abilities. As I mentioned already, music is a tool to assist as part of the transition from one stage of life to another. While these life stages can be stressful and produce anxiety, using music can be the key to managing those emotions as you age, or when working with residents who may be dealing with a tough transition.

MUSICAL RETIREMENT

Improving Exercise and Memory

Another huge benefit that comes with adding music to your routine is that it can help you to get up and move. For you and your loved ones, that movement can be the key to maintaining mobility and independence for a longer period of time. If you currently live in an independent living retirement facility, then adding musical activities can be a way to increase your activity level. Musical exercise classes can be interesting and can motivate you, especially if you might not be into traditional exercise classes.

Recommendations for Activities/Program Managers:

To keep balance in other physical abilities, your residents need to move regularly. Music can be a way to motivate them in this area. When you add music to the routine of your facility, be it a more traditional retirement community or a care facility, you can be contributing to the improvement of your residents' memories.

Research demonstrates that repetitive elements from rhythm and melody can help our brains to form memory-enhancing patterns. For example, stroke survivors were found to benefit from listening to music in terms of verbal memory, reducing their confusion levels, and even helping them to maintain their focus.

Recognize that these benefits can also be shared with you, even if you or your loved ones may not have suffered from a stroke, but still want to maintain memory and mental acuity. Even if you are dealing with other memory issues, then you can benefit, as music therapy can help you to maintain your current mental abilities. This therapy can also help to slow the loss of memory, even if it can't stop the process altogether.

As you can already see, there are a variety of physical and mental benefits that come from adding music as part of your routine. However, one particular benefit is related to addressing physical pain, a problem for many individuals as they age.

Decreasing Physical Pain

The unfortunate reality of aging is addressing pain issues. It could be joints or due to injuries and chronic conditions. Many of you are likely to deal with some form of pain. With music, you now have a tool to address your pain and provide physical comfort. Often, that revolves around taking your mind off of the current situation and instead of helping yourself or your loved ones to focus on memories, especially ones that are joyful or bring back happy moments or events in your lives.

MUSICAL
RETIREMENT

That can help to take your mind off the discomfort you may be dealing with on a daily basis or due to medical procedures.

Research shows that patients recovering from surgery, for example, tend to recover quicker and experience less pain when music is incorporated into their treatment plan. If you are having surgery, such as a knee or hip replacement, then you are likely going to want options to help deal with the pain during your healing process. With music as part of your routine, it can help you to deal with expressing your feelings and coping with various challenges in your life.

Another recent study focused on patients who deal with chronic pain in the form of fibromyalgia, a disease that results in chronic pain in the muscles and joints. After listening to their favorite music, these patients experienced less chronic pain. The researchers see this as a potential way to manage pain, thus potentially helping to reduce the amount of medication that patients may have to take.

The research shows that two brain mechanisms could be responsible for the pain-relieving effect. First, it appears that music might trigger the release of opioids in the brain. Opioids are essentially the body's natural morphine, which may explain why music has an impact on pain. Second, researchers noted that the pain-relieving impact could be a result of redirecting attention away from the source of pain. However, it is interesting to note that the impact of music on pain remains even after the music is no longer playing.

It was also noted that the best impact on pain was achieved when individuals listened to music they like and were already familiar with hearing. My team works with you or your loved ones to help them curate a number of musical options for a variety of situations, including addressing pain or physical discomfort.

For seniors living with similar chronic diseases, these musical options can provide assistance to them, along with their prescribed medications from the doctor. Having musical options can be an additional source of relief for you and your loved ones, something that our musical retirement home will offer.

As you can see, music provides a variety of health benefits, both mentally, emotionally, and physically. Even if it was not part of your life in the past, it doesn't mean that incorporating it into your daily routine won't have benefits in the present. One of the ways that you can incorporate music into your daily routine starts with celebrating your next stage of life.

MUSICAL
RETIREMENT

MUSICAL
RETIREMENT

CHAPTER 5

Birthday Celebrations—
Let's Party!

MUSICAL RETIREMENT

Celebrating birthdays is a fun way to acknowledge how amazing your life is and continues to be. Birthdays are also a time when people tend to reflect on their past experiences, appreciating the wisdom that they have gathered throughout the process. Clearly, there are those who have developed relationships that are dear to their hearts. As you age, it can be difficult to figure out how to celebrate the anniversary of your birth. After all, your interests may have changed, plus your social circle is likely smaller and may be physically challenged. The result is that you may wonder how you can still have a great time even with these challenges.

Keep in mind, as we age, the birthday parties with clowns, balloons, and different kid games become part of the past. Yet the adult birthday parties, where you might have gone out drinking and partying are no longer a fit either. Too often, seniors end up sitting in their rooms or apartments without even a cake to mark the occasion of this special day. Clearly, that can compound feelings of loneliness and isolation.

These types of events are not only marking time but help you to recognize that your life is not over just because you are getting older. It flows back into the idea of helping you to create enjoyment in your life, regardless of any challenges you face.

My goal is to help you find ways to celebrate those special days and to create a positive impact for you and your loved ones while making it fun for family members who attend. Let's get started by creating fun through various activities.

Musical Games at Every Party

One of the first things to do involves getting all the guests and the birthday honoree moving. Musical activities focus on bringing fun to the celebration. Think of fun musical games, such as red light/green light. Adapt them so that all the senior attendees can still participate. The goal of these musical activities is to get them involved, not leaving anyone sitting on the sidelines.

Games, not just the musical ones, are a way to have fun as a group or as an individual. Think of all the different games that use trivia, scavenger hunts, or other mental skills. Those types of games are often included in our birthday parties, simply because they can be easily adapted to any age.

At the same time, I want to point out how important it is that these types of activities can be tailored to any physical limitations of your guests. It is not about making them feel excluded, simply because they might be using a walker or have a wheelchair. Additionally, games can be adapted in terms of the speed at which they are played.

Here is a great example of that type of adaptation. Musical chairs is a game that has been played at various children's parties for decades. That game tends to move fast, with kids trying to hustle in order to get one of the chairs and not be put out at the end of the round.

In a session with your residents, it might be adapted by using a combination of musical chairs and red light/ green light. The idea is that everyone participates to the degree that they can, and has fun doing so. Working with our team, we can find out a bit about you or your loved one who is being celebrated. That process includes learning more about their musical tastes and any potential challenges. Then we adapt the activities to fit their musical tastes and interests while keeping in mind the needs of the guests, including the birthday honoree.

In the end, you are going to enjoy yourself and make more memories with your loved ones, both family and friends.

Being Flexible

Part of the challenges that come with aging is that you might feel great one day and then be struggling with pain and other issues the next day. Hosting a birthday party for an aging loved one means being adaptable. Our team is trained to keep an eye on the room and adapt where necessary. For instance, a game might require a

MUSICAL
RETIREMENT

lot of movement, but if you or your loved one appears to be tired, the activity could be changed to involve sitting instead.

When there is the flexibility to address changes in the environment or mood of the guests, everyone can have a good time and create great memories. I also recognize that hearing loss may impact the crowd. With that in mind, choosing to make shorter speeches might be the best option versus longer speeches that would be a struggle for them to hear or follow along.

The point is to create an experience that is not challenging for the guest of honor. Be prepared to shift locations if necessary, bringing the party inside if the original plan was outside but the weather got too hot or too chilly for your guest of honor.

What are Their Interests? Recommendations for Seniors

Another part of planning a birthday party is to adapt the event to the hobbies and interests of the guest of honor. Is there a particular activity they have always enjoyed? Could you make that the theme of the event?

Create musical activities that focus around that theme, allowing everyone attending the party to also explore and learn more about the birthday honoree's hobbies and interests. The point is to personalize the event. The party is about celebrating your guest of honor and the long life that they have lived, as well as their accumulated wisdom.

However, you are not limited to just musical games but can incorporate puzzles, video games, and even card or dice games, depending on the interests of your guest list. Notice that the theme around these types of games is that they can be played or enjoyed around a table. Plus, these types of games encourage conversation or "table talk" as the players socialize.

Board games also have the added benefit of contributing to a slowing of cognitive decline. Socializing can be a great way to combat depression, especially as individuals age. If you are trying to get multiple generations engaged at a birthday party, use tabletop games to engage everyone. Think of a spirited card game, which can be played tournament style. Everyone is moving seats, and conversations are constantly being started and encouraged. The point of these types of activities is to make the birthday party fun and enjoyable for everyone.

There are also a variety of traditional party games that can be adapted to fit into the theme of the birthday party. Piñatas are a favorite for kids, and with a few adaptations in how the piñata was made, it can be a great game for seniors as well. Use brown paper wrapping cut into shapes that can be glued or stapled together. The game can be fun, and the brown wrapping is easier to break open.

Trivia games can also be fun, tapping into the

MUSICAL
RETIREMENT

knowledge that seniors have accumulated over the years. Everyone will end up fighting for a senior partner, as they are a treasure trove of information. You might even be able to adapt the game to focus on a specific decade, or even create questions based entirely on the lives of those who are playing the game, including family members of the guest of honor. It personalizes the trivia game, plus everyone can get involved in making questions prior to the start of the game.

If a majority of those attending were together during a specific event or period of time, then you can create questions around that event. The point is to make it fun for everyone attending, and to show that senior how much they are loved by family and friends.

Bingo is a game that is often associated with aging in many parts of the world. Halls are devoted to the game on a weekly basis, and people might have multiple bingo cards in front of them. It is a game that allows people to chat while they are playing and can be played by individuals regardless of their physical activity level. The prizes can be related to different hobbies of the guest of honor, or just fun and silly prizes. Younger guests can help to decorate or make the bingo cards.

With a fun and energetic bingo caller, the game can draw everyone in. Plus, it can be adapted in multiple ways, so everyone can enjoy the benefits of a fun and spirited game. Scavenger hunts can also get everyone involved by creating teams that pair younger and older guests together. Our team is focused on finding ways to involve all the guests at the party. The point is to celebrate a life and create new memories in the process. For instance, use various musical props to get all the guests involved, from children to adults. There are wooden sticks and instruments that anyone can use regardless of their musical ability. Everyone also plays with different styles of music. Those who are participating can also take turns being the conductor of this impromptu orchestra. This is a part of the party that I personally love, and so do the guests.

Our team can work with you to create an amazing experience for the senior you are celebrating. Contact us at https://www.musicalretirement.com to learn more about our birthday parties and how we can make your event a special one!

Ultimately, the key to a great senior birthday party is to start planning your party early. If everything is confirmed well in advance, then you can make adjustments as needed and make things go smoothly. The benefits of working with my team are that you can have an amazing party, and we will help walk you through the process. At my musical retirement facility, we also offer a variety of options for you and your loved ones to celebrate their birthdays in high style.

Celebrations are great, but the reality is that this celebration is only held once a year. Throughout the rest of the year, seniors face a variety of challenges, both physical and emotional. That level of stress could compound different physical ailments of seniors,

MUSICAL
RETIREMENT

meaning that connections with others are key to helping them manage it.

Since you may be dealing with those challenges, it can create a high level of stress. In the next chapter, I want to focus on various ways to help relieve stress, which can be implemented into seniors' daily lives, plus enjoy the benefits when you take the time to address the causes of seniors' stress.

MUSICAL
RETIREMENT

CHAPTER 6

Eleven Tips to Reduce Stress in Your Senior Years

An unfortunate part of life is that there will always be stressful situations to deal with. For seniors, dealing with stress can be even more complicated, because your traditional stress relievers might no longer be around. Supportive circles of people might no longer be there, making it harder for seniors to then deal with the stress that they face.

Plus, there are the physical challenges that come with age, bringing their own unique stressors, both mentally and emotionally. With this unique challenge of dealing with stress in mind, here are eleven tips that you can use to deal with the various levels of stress seniors may encounter during the aging process.

1. Get Moving

The importance of exercise and moving as we age cannot be understated. Putting physical stress on your body through exercise actually helps you to relieve mental stress. At the same time, it is a great way to maintain your physical abilities, including balance and range of motion.

How does exercise help you to reduce stress? One, exercise lowers your stress hormones over a longer period of time, while releasing endorphins, the chemicals that improve your mood and also serve as natural painkillers. Plus, when you are exercising, it improves the quality of your sleep. This is a real benefit, especially when you are stressed and not sleeping well.

Most of the benefits of exercise will come from consistency. You are likely to enjoy a greater confidence and mental well-being when you are able to exercise regularly. As a musical facility, the best way to promote any exercise routine is through engaging activities that encourage movement, thus disguising exercise in something fun.

Musical activities, for instance, get you and/or your loved ones moving in a fun way. It gives everyone a chance to get active. Other options that we can offer include exercise classes that promote flexibility, such as yoga or Pilates, modified for seniors at any age. Activities that are fun and provide exercise can also incorporate fun outside hobbies, such as garden walks or dancing. These offerings can allow you to focus on getting active, and thus reducing your stress levels.

2. Consider Supplements

Part of the reality of aging involves recognizing that your body is no longer going to provide all the hormones and regulators you need to function. When hormones are out of balance, it can increase your levels of stress and anxiety. One way to manage that stress and anxiety is through supplements.

The following supplements are known for their ability to promote stress and anxiety reduction. Here are a few of the options available, although any supplements need to be reviewed with your doctor, thus making sure that they are not going to negatively interact with your current medications.

- **Lemon balm**—A member of the mint family, lemon balm has been studied for its anti-anxiety effects.

- **Ashwagandha**—An herb used in Ayurvedic medicine, it treats stress and anxiety, with several studies pointing to its efficacy.

- **Green tea**—This tea is very popular right now for a variety of reasons, including its polyphenol antioxidants, which are known for their health benefits. Research points to the fact that green tea appears to increase serotonin levels, which can lower anxiety and stress.

- **Valerian root**—A popular sleep aid, it contains valerenic acid, which alters GABA receptors and lowers anxiety.

- **Kava kava**—This member of the pepper family is used in Europe and the U.S. to treat mild stress and anxiety.

As I said, these are just a few of the supplement options available. Again, it is important to check with your physician or encourage your loved ones to do so, before adding any supplements to a daily routine. The goal of adding them will be to feed your body, allowing you to enjoy your life to the fullest.

3. Candles or Essential Oils

Scents can have a powerful impact on your mind and body. Many essential oils, or candles made with essential oils, can have an impact. After all, many different scents can be associated with positive memories, which can reduce stress and anxiety.

Here are a few of the scents that you might consider using in your rooms. All of them are known for their soothing qualities, including reducing stress or anxiety.

- Lavender

- Rose

- Frankincense

- Sandalwood

- Orange blossom

- Geranium

- Ylang ylang

- Roman chamomile

- Bergamot

Using scents can promote aromatherapy, which can help to reduce stress and anxiety, as well as promote a good night's sleep.

4. Reducing Caffeine Options for Residents

While caffeine is considered a common part of life, particularly as a pick-me-up, the reality is that high doses of caffeine can contribute to higher levels of anxiety and stress. Caffeine is often found in coffee, tea, chocolate, and energy drinks. Since everyone has different levels of tolerance to caffeine, some may be able to enjoy it more than others.

Consider cutting back if you notice increased levels of anxiety and stress. It might also help to look for alternative drink options, including flavored water or juices. The point is to reduce your stress levels by limiting caffeine.

5. Take the Time to Journal

During times of stress and anxiety, seniors need to find outlets to deal with it. One of those is journaling. The point is to help you bring your feelings and thoughts out into the open. Once you get them out of your head, it can be easier to address them.

To assist yourself in this process, make items available that help in your journaling. The process of journaling can be done either by writing or by recording your thoughts. Look for journals that offer writing prompts, such as what you are grateful for. When you focus on gratitude, then it can help to change your mindset and reduce your stress and anxiety levels.

Those writing prompts can help you to get started, and once you start writing, you might be surprised at how quickly the thoughts and feelings start pouring out of your mind and heart.

6. Encourage Connections with Family and Friends

Our facility does a lot to maintain residents' connections with family and friends. Social support can be the key to dealing with a variety of challenges, including stress and anxiety. Encouraging these visits and social occasions by making them a key part of our routine is a vital part of who we are.

It might include family dinners during the week, or other activities where families and friends are welcomed. The point is that friendship, be it with family or close friends, can be a beneficial way to release oxytocin, a natural stress reliever. Men and women with limited social connections tend to be more likely to suffer from stress and anxiety, as well as depression. Continuing social relationships and building connections between residents can be a big help in addressing stress and anxiety.

Tend and befriend is the opposite of the flight and fight response. That fight or flight response is often associated with increased levels of stress and anxiety. Therefore, anything that encourages you to befriend others is ultimately going to positively impact you.

7. Laughing and Finding Joy

Music is a great way to bring joy into your life. Songs can bring back positive memories, but the music itself has the power to get your feet moving and your mood lifted. When you are looking to increase your joy, music can be a way to do so. Often, funny songs are meant to satire various life events or aspects of a culture.

Playing those songs as part of your activities, or just making those recordings available, can help you and your loved ones to laugh and have fun. It can be a huge way to lift the mood and reduce stress or anxiety. Plus, it can relieve tension in the muscles, allowing you to relax. Laughter can also help to improve your immune system as well.

Laughter is a tool to deal with various aspects of changing health and physical circumstances. A study

MUSICAL RETIREMENT

among cancer patients found that those who participated in a laughter intervention group experienced more stress relief than those who were just distracted. The goal is to bring joy into your life, whether it is through music, comedy shows, or anything that encourages laughter. The point is to enjoy the benefits of laughter and joy, thus helping to reduce stress levels.

8. Encourage Animal Interactions

There are so many relaxing benefits of interactions with animals, be it with pets or therapy animals. Create opportunities for yourself to interact with animals. In your garden areas, you might put bird houses or other enticements that draw them, and thus allow you or your loved one to enjoy observing them. Thus, you can get the benefits of enjoying these animals with minimal efforts.

However, if you are looking for more deliberate interactions, then you might also take advantage of animal rescues that want to acclimate dogs and cats to human interactions. The point is to give yourself a chance to deal with animals and enjoy their relaxing benefits. However, it is also important to make sure that you take into account any allergies before bringing animals into your area.

9. Taking a Yoga Class

While I talked about yoga classes in previous chapters, it is important to note how critical they can be in helping you to clear your head. Plus, this form of exercise can be adapted to all age groups. That means, even with limited mobility, you can still enjoy the benefits of yoga.

The point of yoga is to achieve the goal of joining the mind and body. This goal is achieved by helping individuals achieve greater awareness of their body and breathing. Therefore, the focus on breathing and clearing the mind allows stress to leave the mind and body, even if it is just for a short period of time.

Yoga can also help to reduce mental stress by focusing on deep breathing in a mindful way. Deep breathing exercises activate the parasympathetic nervous system, which controls your relaxation response. There are several types of deep breathing exercises, many of which have been incorporated into various yoga classes.

Lowering your stress level, even temporarily, can also help you to find a solution to deal with what is causing your stress. While you or a loved one might not share the reason for being stressed, a yoga class can still be an outlet to deal with it in a positive way.

Overall, research has found that yoga enhances mood while also lowering cortisol levels, blood pressure, and heart rate. While there are still questions regarding how

MUSICAL
RETIREMENT

yoga actually reduces stress, the reality is that many individuals talk about its benefits.

10. Meditation

For many seniors, meditation is a simple practice that anyone can master, regardless of age or physical ability. One of the primary benefits of meditation is how it can help individuals to reduce stress, increase internal calmness and clarity, and promote happiness. With all the benefits, you might be wondering how to get started. The truth is that learning to meditate is straightforward, with almost immediate benefits.

What happens when you meditate? As you begin to meditate, your autonomic nervous system is activated, centering your body's energy and helping you to find balance.

To get started, find a quiet place where you can close your eyes and focus on your breathing. During that process, you also quiet your thoughts, simply allowing yourself to just be. The process can be very relaxing and comforting. Even just a few minutes on a daily basis can make a big difference in your level of mental and physical discomfort. For seniors, this can be just one more tool to help them deal with their emotions, as well as chronic physical conditions.

Why does meditation have such a positive impact? Primarily because it helps your body to release anxiety and stress. When you are dealing with anxiety, your breath quickens, the body tightens up, and arteries start to narrow. Once you start feeling bad physically, your anxiety continues to increase. Meditation can help you to break the anxiety cycle.

However, meditation is not just to address physical discomfort. It can be a time when you focus on your dreams and take time to think about your present and your future. Meditation can also help you quiet your mind during difficult situations, such as moving, the loss of a partner, or the loss of friends. As a senior, there are also additional benefits from meditation. Here are just a few of them:

- **Chronic pain reduction**—Meditation, along with yoga, can help to build muscle strength and support damaged joints, thus improving your pain management.

- **Stress reduction**—As I have already mentioned, meditation provides relaxation techniques that can decrease stress. It also increases blood flow throughout the body, which can be beneficial for those dealing with dementia or early onset Alzheimer's.

- **Uplifting mood**—Depression is a reality for many individuals as they face change and loss during the aging process. Meditating can help them to manage their feelings and positively

MUSICAL
RETIREMENT

impact their depression and anxiety, as well as to better handle changes throughout their lives.

- **Managing Hypertension and Diabetes**— Meditation, along with yoga or other exercise routines, can assist in managing hypertension. How? By helping individuals become better at regulating their breathing, contributing to a more relaxed physical state. Relieving stress can also help with managing diabetes, along with yoga poses meant to improve blood flow.

As a senior, the benefits of meditation make it worth becoming part of your daily routine at any age.

11. Listening to Soothing Music

While I have repeatedly pointed out the benefits of music and therapies that involve music, there is something to be said for the stress relief that comes from listening to soothing music when your mind is troubled. Slow-paced music, such as instrumentals, classical, Native American, Indian, or Celtic, can be soothing to the mind and spirit.

The body responds to this type of music by lowering blood pressure and heart rate, as well as decreasing stress hormones. However, you can also bring those soothing benefits through areas devoted to nature. After all, if you have created gardens that attract birds and other wildlife, then you create places where you can enjoy nature sounds.

Those types of sounds are often incorporated in relaxation and meditation music.

Our team can work with you to create a library of music to provide a variety of musical options. Plus, we can also make recommendations based on any challenges that you might be facing.

The point is that by making this musical library available, seniors can enjoy the benefits of music, regardless of the activities. After all, music can be incorporated with arts and crafts, as well as gardening, or even just playing in the background while residents read and journal.

One of the important aspects of incorporating music into every area of your life is the connection that it can create between the past and present. To understand how that connection occurs, I want to talk about the importance of music in various cultures.

MUSICAL
RETIREMENT

MUS CAL
RET REMENT

CHAPTER 7

The Cultural Connection
with Music

MUSICAL RETIREMENT

Music is truly wrapped up in many cultures throughout the world. In many cultures, music is associated with enlightenment, connection with a higher power, or is even a key part of creating a deeper connection with yourself. For many seniors, cultural and religious connections to music resonate with their faith and spirituality. Here I explore the various musical elements found in the religions that I have encountered during my nursing career and my work with seniors.

In **Christianity**, music is a critical part of worship. Hymns and the chorus are seen as part of any church service. That musical connection speaks to history within the Bible, where music was part of the daily routine of the lives of early Christians. The Psalms are full of songs written throughout the ages, talking about the glory of God and the importance of his service.

Even weddings, baptisms, and funerals, within the Christian faith, have songs as part of these events, making the connection between the religious event and your spirituality. The result is that songs of faith can be used by individuals to help them deal with stress and challenges. Seniors may have their favorite hymns or other music that helps them to draw closer to their faith. The **Muslim** religion, one of the largest in the world, also includes music in its rituals. However, the musical expression is very diverse, simply because the religion exists across multiple ethnicities. Many religious songs are sung without the use of any musical instruments. Singing moral songs without music is considered permissible by those of the Muslim faith, although there are some musical instruments that may be used for devotional music.

Other music may be used throughout their culture, provided that it is not associated with a religious service. There are songs of praise to Allah and Muhammad, as well as songs of praise that are associated with Sufi music. Again, the beauty of this culture is that it incorporates the music and ethnic backgrounds of everyone who adheres to the Muslim faith.

In the **Jewish** culture, music is part of worship, part of rituals regarding moving into adulthood, and part of each phase of life, from marriage to babies. There are traditions of religious music that are sung as part of time at the synagogue and during prayers, as well as secular music. What makes the Jewish musical tradition so interesting is that being Jewish is ethnicity and a religion, so the music reflects that.

Differences in rhythm and sound can be found among different Jewish communities. From the beginning of the Jewish people, music was part of their temple routine. The regular temple orchestra included twelve different instruments and twelve male members of a choir. Versions of that type of public singing have continued, even after the temple was destroyed by the Babylonians and the dispersion of the Jews throughout the Middle East and Europe.

Today, the cantor is seen as a key part of the musical experience of the Jewish faith. The cantor will sing a half-verse at a time, while the congregation sings a refrain back. The congregation may also repeat what the cantor had already sung. Another option is for the cantor to sing one verse and the congregation to sing the alternative verses. All of these aspects of the modern musical tradition in the Jewish faith draw on the musical roots of these unique people.

Another faith with a deep connection to music is **Buddhism**, which is deeply connected to chanting. By doing the chanting in a musical rhythm, it allows you to clear your mind and let go of your concerns and worries. The point is to bring peace into your mind and heart. You might be thinking, where is the connection to music? As you listen to chanting, it becomes a song and its own music. The beauty of a voice chanting and contributing to the peace of a mind and heart is a beautiful form of music all its own.

Now, there are other cultures that also have musical connections throughout their history. I can think of the **Native Americans** and how music was the key to a successful hunt, to their connection with nature, and to religious ceremonies. I find it interesting that in culture after culture, region after region, there are musical ties and connections.

The **Asian culture** encompasses the musical culture of Arabia, Central Asia, East Asia, South Asia, and Southeast Asia. That means there are a variety of musical compositions using stringed instruments, often associated with different dances for entertainment and for religious purposes.

China is a country that has a large population and a rich musical history. The classical music often associated with China built its cultural base over three thousand years. What makes this cultural music stand out is its unique systems of musical notation and a scale with twelve notes to an octave. Imagine how someone, who may have immigrated away from China, would feel hearing the music of their homeland. That emotional tie cannot be broken, even if you make a significant life change.

The activities regarding music in any culture can often start with the creation of the music itself. The process of building and creating music means building connections between leaders and artists in a variety of communities and cultures. Music becomes part of the art of that culture, often taking on great significance. Ancient philosophers in both Greece and India defined music as tones that were ordered both horizontally and vertically. Depending on the culture, newer forms of music can be seen as "not being music." For instance, today, Beethoven's Grosse Fuge string quartet is now considered a classical piece of music, but when

Beethoven wrote it, the piece was seen as not truly being music.

Jazz, in the early years, was seen as a violation of everything that was part of the American culture in the early 1900s. Parents and others in authority protested jazz, even as the young people embraced it. Today, jazz is seen as a fundamental part of many other types of music, including rap and hip hop. My point here is that time can make a type of music appealing, and a part of the culture, allowing it to end up defining a generation.

If you have lived many years on this earth, you likely have songs or music that connects you to your youth or specific events. Music may have even been a hobby of yours, as you played in the orchestra or band at school. Some of you may have even started your own band with friends, playing for the neighborhood in the garage of your parents' home.

Part of the reason that I shared these examples with you is that they demonstrate the cultural significance that you might have with different types of music. As you have aged, certain music associated with your culture and history may have disappeared from your life.

To me, that disappearance of such emotionally charged music means that you have severed a connection with your past, a part of yourself that defines who you are, as well as your beliefs and values.

How can a musical retirement home help to renew that connection?

The Beauty of Culture

The first thing to note is that everyone brings their cultural influences with them into all areas of their lives. It is not just a type of music that you listen to strictly for pleasure. Think of how certain cultural musical pieces can recall critical moments in your life. For example, when a Jewish young man looks back at his bar mitzvah, then he might also recall some of the music played that day. Any time that he hears music with a similar beat or tune, he may be drawn back to that memory or place in time. It is a connection with his past that can bring comfort to him in his present.

Focus on bringing those musical cultural influences into your daily routine. I find that by bringing in those musical pieces for seniors, you can make a connection with people and rituals that you love.

The knowledge and wisdom gained from a lifetime of experience is not something you should dismiss. By connecting with seniors with their youth through culture music references, then you provide the gift of bridging the gap between you then and you now.

Getting older doesn't mean that your youth is not a part of you. Sitting with a staff member at my musical retirement facility means that you will enjoy the benefit of connecting with your youth and culture, bringing them with you into the present.

Avoid Feelings of Loneliness

This point is especially important in light of the reality that aging, and the loss of loved ones, can bring a level of loneliness. As you age, it can be challenging to remain positive and not fall prey to loneliness. Connecting with your culture can be a way to combat the loneliness. It can help to ground you into a world that is familiar and comforting.

Think of all the ways that we attach sentimentality to objects, not because of the object itself, but what that object represents within our past. In fact, as seniors prepare to downsize into a retirement facility, it can feel overwhelming to decide which of your treasured possessions is going to make the move, and which ones are going to a new home.

What makes music so nice is that it doesn't take up a lot of space and can go just about anywhere. That means seniors can enjoy the beauty of the music, the sentiment from the past, and bring that joy into your present. While other objects can have ties to your past, music can have ties to your past or with your loved ones, as well as your present.

Building new friendships and social connections through your cultural ties and music can be a great way

MUSICAL
RETIREMENT

to combat loneliness. Those new friendships can help you to enjoy this next season of your life, instead of longing for a past that is no longer part of your life.

I keep bringing up the importance of the cultural representations of music because I have found that there is joy in connecting with where you came from and where you are right now. Embracing your culture can be a way to connect with something inside yourself.

Plus, as you age, your cultural connections can often help you to deal with the fact that more of your life is in your rear-view mirror. Questions about death and what happens afterwards may be found in your religious rituals, which include music. Hearing music related to those aspects of your personal spirituality can be a comfort for you as you age.

Your personal faith can be bolstered by your musical and cultural connections. Think of how much joy you feel when you hear a specific song or gospel related to your religious background. It is uplifting and, for many individuals, it can help them to get through challenging situations.

Clearly, the point of culture and music is part of what we are building in our musical retirement home. It is a chance for you to explore your culture and religious past, bringing back what comforts you, but also the joy associated with those aspects of your past.

However, as part of our musical routine, I don't want to just talk about music and how it can help your mood or give you a chance to rebuild a cultural connection. Instead, I want to focus on how music and exercise can be combined to create an amazing experience as you age.

MUSICAL
RETIREMENT

MUSICAL
RETIREMENT

CHAPTER 8

Program Managers
Introduce Musical
Exercises for Seniors

MUSICAL RETIREMENT

One of the challenges for seniors is the fact that their mobility decreases, and their balance is impacted. Exercise and being active is a great way to help manage a senior's mobility and balance. I find that exercising helps to slow that decrease, while also helping to maintain their independence for a longer period of time.

When you are trying to keep your residents healthy, activities that promote their physical well-being are often the best. What is nice about these activities is that they often don't have to cost much, yet their benefits can be huge.

With seniors, finding ways to bring in exercise and movement through less traditional methods is the key. Musical exercise classes can be a way to bring in movement and activity through a fun and engaging method. Plus, musical exercises can be adapted to meet the different fitness levels of your residents.

Part of the goal of these exercises is to give seniors a sense of control over their lives and their mobility. They may not always realize the benefits of the exercises, but in the end, seniors will be able to feel them.

Throughout the next few pages, I want to share some of the musical exercises that our team uses to create enjoyable activities for seniors.

Dance Classes

In today's world, dance classes have become exercise classes. The goal is to get people moving without necessarily being conscious of how they look in the process. These classes are focused on getting people to move and have fun while doing so.

Think of the ways that exercise has evolved into just moving your body in ways that feel comfortable. Dance classes, especially ones that have more of a free flow, give people the chance to move in the ways that they are comfortable with.

Choosing dance classes for seniors is also a great way to bring exercise into their routine without billing it as real exercise. It is similar to disguising vegetables in dishes that are fun to eat. You enjoy it and also pass on benefits to seniors.

With that in mind, look for dance studios and instructors that would be willing to come to you, either at a facility or a senior community center. When you bring musical classes to the senior community, you can make it easier for them to enjoy these aspects of their lives. The point is to get them excited to attend the classes and keep them moving. It is a great way to focus on continual mobility.

Another form of musical exercise classes can involve using drums or other hand-held instruments as part of the movements of the class. Cardio drumming classes, for example, use drumsticks, balls, and tubs or laundry baskets as part of the exercise routine. You take advantage of the rhythm, allowing seniors to exercise while playing together. Our team frequently brings in these types of instruments as part of our activities, encouraging regular participation from the seniors that we work with, both in our facility and in other facilities that request our services.

Seniors can either sit or stand while beating their drum. You might use yoga balls or beach balls, along with a container to hold the ball. Notice that you don't necessarily have to invest in high-priced drum kits to enjoy the drumming benefits available.

Another benefit is that you can use upbeat songs as part of the routine. That gives seniors a great arm workout, but it also increases their cardio workout. Plus, upbeat songs have a positive impact on their mood, giving all the residents a mood lift before they leave the event.

As you can see, both of these exercise class options are focused on increasing participation through movement and rhythm. Now let's translate this into more musically focused events.

High Participation Musical Classes

There are a variety of ways to create musical classes. It might involve lessons to teach a unique instrument. However, you can also use bells to have your residents

MUSICAL
RETIREMENT

chime in at particular points during a song. The point is to use simple instruments to increase participation and thus get your residents excited to attend. Our team uses participation to make our events more interesting and entertaining for those in attendance. Plus, seniors hear from their friends about how fun it was, and that frequently plays a part in building attendance.

Think about how much more you enjoy learning about something when you get to actively participate. The goal is to increase their participation to the point that they are excited about that activity. When you have excited seniors, then you will see it in your attendance numbers. Trying to determine what activities to fund comes down to the numbers and the benefits for the seniors in your community. Ideally, you are going to find the perfect balance in the events offered by my team, but you may also find others that inspire your residents.

Various senior activities can be led by community members, but you can also opt to hire professional musicians, such as the ones working with my team. Our professional musicians are focused on using drums and other percussion instruments to get seniors active.

Xylophones are another option that can give seniors a chance to participate in the playing of a song. Along the way, you can teach them their musical scales, introducing them to musical notes. As a part of the activity, you can tap each of the bars and explain which notes you are playing.

These instruments are not typically included in

traditional songs, so your residents can still hear the other instruments that they are complementing with the xylophone. Our team encourages those attending to play the lower or higher notes, depending on the songs.

If your residents have trouble holding onto instruments, wrist bells are another way to allow them to participate. You might even include arm exercises with the bells, getting them to work on their arm strength as they lift and shake the bells to the music.

Notice that all of these participation classes are going to get everyone involved, and can also be easily adapted to fit the current physical abilities of the seniors attending. That means you can create participation classes that challenge everyone and get them excited to attend.

Maracas are another option to try. I find it interesting that certain instruments also tend to connect in people's minds with specific types of music. You can incorporate maracas with Latin or Caribbean music, for example. Another way to make maracas a part of several activities is to buy plain maracas and then have a creative craft project. Once your residents have finished decorating them, you can start the musical activity.

If you want to make your own maracas, then simply fill a few prescription bottles with dried beans or rice. Now you are ready to get musical!

You might even be able to do a conga line as part of your musical adventure.

Another activity is one that focuses on laughter.

MUSICAL
RETIREMENT

After all, laughter is associated with so many physical and mental benefits. Plus, laughing is something that we can do regardless of age and mobility. One of the ways that our team incorporates laughter through music is by using songs with funny lyrics that bring to mind silly pictures or fun memories.

Can you imagine how many good belly laughs a song can bring to a group of seniors? We encourage laughs, regardless of how they come. It might be in funny faces that we make to the music or the games we play. The point is to allow them to find joy through music and laughter. The quality of life can be improved so much, simply by taking the time to add laughter and music into your daily activities.

There are so many ways to get seniors involved in these musical activities, but the best part is that you are showing that a senior's life can actually improve. With that in mind, let's turn to how my team can help you to incorporate music more fully into your facility. The next chapter outlines a few of the options retirement homes and care facilities can take advantage of for their seniors.

MUSICAL
RETIREMENT

CHAPTER 9

Learning How to Incorporate Music into Your Facility

MUSICAL RETIREMENT

No matter if you are the activity director or manager of a retirement facility, you are likely always looking for ways to bring enjoyment into the lives of your residents. My belief is that music is a way to bring that enjoyment to your residents, from those who are still living independently to those who are aging in place at your facility.

With that in mind, part of the journey of your facility is determining the areas that you are doing well in, meeting the needs of your residents, and identifying how music can make the experience of meeting their needs even better. The point of incorporating music is to build an amazing experience for your seniors. With that in mind, I want to focus on giving your seniors some amazing experiences over a longer period of time.

Here are a few of the senior seminars I offer, and some of the activities involved in our process. Look at these seminars as a way to jump-start the introduction of musical activities into your facility.

One-Day Musical Seminar for Seniors

Right from the start of my seminars, I emphasize the ways to bring enjoyment into the lives of your residents.

My goal is to give your seniors some musical tools that contribute to your musical culture. That starts by doing homework about your facility even before I arrive. I want to know about the type of activities that get your seniors up and moving. What draws your residents into an activity and gives them a joyful experience? My seminars are going to give your residents musical components to increase their joy and quality of life.

The point of adding musical attributes is about creating more value in what is already going well in your facility. You want to keep drawing residents and their families who are looking for activities that are going to help their loved ones remain active and upbuild. Your choices of activities and options contribute to the atmosphere of your facility, giving a positive impression to potential residents and their families. One of those activities can be our one-day musical seminar for seniors.

This seminar focuses on our coaching for seniors, teaching them how music can benefit them throughout the day, and helping them to recognize that they are still responsible for their quality of life and joy.

As part of a one-day seminar, our team can demonstrate various musical activities that we offer in our facility. That can help you determine which ones you might want to consider adding to your facility. With our team, you can also offer seminars that provide activities for seniors over several days. Our two and three-day seminars each offer different aspects, which I will now share.

Two to Three-Day Musical Seminar for Seniors

My seminars focus on how to increase the quality of the lives of your residents through music. I base them on three areas where you can incorporate music more fully into their lives. In my two-day seminars, I tend to incorporate the coaching from my one-day seminar, across the two-day period, along with specific activities designed to get your seniors moving and motivated.

The first day of the seminar is a session focused on sharing the benefits of music in your daily life. I encourage seniors to share their favorite music and how it makes them feel. These early sessions are meant to get your seniors comfortable with my team.

Next, we start moving into more coaching, combined with various musical activities. Many of the activities that my team can bring to your facility are focused on creating an interactive experience with the audience. As I draw them into the experience, they have a fun time that they tell others about.

Let me be clear. Anyone can stand in front of an audience and play a song or shake a tambourine. Using members of my team, you benefit from trained musicians who have perfected their craft of entertaining and connecting with their audience.

As you have learned through these chapters, music has many benefits for seniors. Therefore, implementing musical activities in the correct way will guarantee that your residents enjoy those benefits for years to come.

Purchasing a two-day seminar for your residents allows you to see a variety of musical activities, thus giving your activity director a chance to see what appeals to your residents and what can be expanded upon.

My three-day seminar option focuses on incorporating music lessons. I can share with your seniors the benefits of music lessons and share with your team how to find instruments and qualified teachers. At the end of the three-day seminar, you and your seniors have the foundation for setting up a music program for residents looking to learn an instrument or explore their creativity through music.

Setting up these programs can be done in a budget-friendly manner while focusing on how to make the right connections to meet the needs of those residents who are interested in these lessons. Plus, you can also showcase what those residents have learned, through a concert program for the other residents.

Another option for your three-day program is to incorporate musical exercise classes into our senior coaching versus musical lessons. With that in mind, you can combine the mental and physical benefits of music for your residents. It can become the basis of an exercise program that incorporates music with movement. If your staff wants to continue to program past the three-day seminar, my team can help your staff to connect with additional community resources.

One of the important things that I have recognized over the years is that it can be challenging to keep seniors moving, especially as they start to have complications related to their balance.

Combining music and exercise can be a way to overcome that barrier for your residents and keep them moving. My seminars focus on how you can network to grow the musical options in your facility and create an amazing experience for your residents.

Beyond the Seminars–
Creating Musical Experiences

Part of exploring music can involve sharing different musical experiences with your residents. Creating a concert program could involve bringing in musicians to play for residents.

Each seminar allows you to bring amazing musical activities to your residents, and to grow a program that fits the needs of your residents. I also hope to inspire you to look within your community and build a network to positively impact the lives of your residents.

My vision for musical retirement is focused on building an amazing and joyful experience for seniors. I want them to be able to create enjoyment in their lives, regardless of the physical and mental challenges that they may be dealing with.

Right at the start, I showcased the ideal day in a musical retirement home. Notice that from the moment they awoke, music was part of their daily routine.

MUSICAL
RETIREMENT

I made it part of waking up, getting ready, meals, daily activities, therapy, and even the nighttime routine. There are a variety of ways to incorporate music, and each of the chapters in this book focused on different areas where music could be part of the lives of seniors, both those still living independently and those who have moved into a retirement facility.

Our team provides a variety of ways to include music and can serve as a guide to help families and facility directors, even if you are not looking to incorporate music into every aspect of the daily routine. You might want to start out with a few areas and then build from there.

My dream was to create a retirement facility that fully integrated music into all of its aspects. With that goal realized, I recognize that there are seniors throughout the world who could benefit from music right now. My facility can serve as a model for other retirement facilities around the world.

However, you do not need a musical facility to reap the benefits.

Now I want you to start going through this book and highlighting the opportunities you see to make the seniors in your life utilize music in their daily routine.

If you are an activity director, think about all the inspiration available for you and your facility to grow your musical activities.

Granted, not every senior is going to want to participate in every musical activity that you offer.

Still, they can benefit from the variety of options found within this book. Perhaps one senior is interested in music lessons, while another enjoys a musical exercise program. Both are benefiting from the musical offerings available in their facility or local community center.

Opening your mind to music means focusing on the enjoyment of the seniors in your life and putting it right at the forefront of their daily activities. Creating an amazing experience can get seniors to share their experiences with family members and friends. For activity directors, these experiences can lead to a positive reputation in the community. What does that positive reputation do for your facility?

The experiences of your seniors now will be what continues to draw residents to your facility in the future. Remember, all retirement facilities offer activities and exercise classes, but incorporating music can make your facility stand out.

Granted, your facility may offer a variety of options that make it appealing already. However, no business grows without being open to opportunities. Incorporating aspects of musical retirement involves looking at what you do now and how you can bring greater enjoyment and benefits to your residents.

My focus is on expanding the enjoyment of retirement through music and opening facilities dedicated to music. Yet, as you have read, your whole facility does not have to be musical to benefit from musical activities. I would love to work with your team and your seniors to help

MUSICAL
RETIREMENT

you find ways to bring music into your facility. Contact me at musicalretirement.com to find out how we can work together.

In the meantime, keep dancing and bringing music into the lives of the seniors in your world. It can truly create an amazing quality of life throughout their senior years!

With that in mind, let's talk about how important appreciating music can be at any age, and how it can contribute to a better overall quality of life.

MUSICAL
RETIREMENT

CHAPTER 10

Appreciating Music
at Any Age

MUSICAL RETIREMENT

The beauty of music is that it can connect with you at all ages. No matter where you are in your life, or the challenges that you might be dealing with, music can be a constant source of encouragement and emotional solace. At some point, however, it seems as if music slips out of our lives, and we lose that connection. It could be that technology has filled our lives with so many distractions, which ultimately results in disconnection. Yet, for seniors, technology connects them with the people, music, and activities that they enjoyed in their youth. Those seniors who can remember a time without smartphones and tablets are learning to use this technology to maintain connections with their families.

The benefits of technology also extend to helping seniors reconnect with their musical favorites. Along the way, they might be introduced to some new musical artists to enjoy as well. Musical appreciation is about connecting with others through music, and also connecting with yourself. Let's talk about how music can benefit your residents, regardless of the stage of life they might find themselves at, and how appreciating music brings enjoyment to their lives.

Finding Joy in Musical Appreciation

The benefits of music, both physically and mentally, have been pointed out throughout these chapters. My passion for music is such that I can't imagine not finding ways to share it with others. One of the ways that I believe in sharing music with others is through teaching an instrument.

While I have talked about the benefits of listening to music and moving to music, there is another aspect where your residents can benefit. That is learning how to play and create with a musical instrument. When you begin the process of learning a musical instrument, several aspects of your brain begin to engage in the process.

Your level of focus and concentration increases as a result. I think of it as fine-tuning your brain, simply because your concentration needs to be sharper. Can you see how that could translate into other areas of your residents' lives? The beauty of playing music is that it can also spark the creativity of your residents.

Clearly, it can become a part of the activities that your facility offers. There could be beginner classes for those looking to learn a new instrument. Wind instruments can not only be fun to learn, but also have the added benefit of improving their respiratory system. Encouraging residents to learn a wind instrument can help them to keep breathing deeply and maintain their lung capacity, even as they face the physical challenges of aging.

Then there is the fact that the seniors are now memorizing notes, keeping the beat, and following the tempo of the musical piece they are learning. All of these aspects are going to be great for improving and sharpening your memory.

The benefits of learning an instrument are going to have the greatest impact when it is part of a regular routine. That includes not only lessons but opportunities to practice through regular sessions. Music lessons and practice sessions are also a great way to increase opportunities for social interactions between residents.

However, once you start getting a few musically talented residents, they have the chance to take on more complicated musical pieces. These pieces can be challenging, but think of the sense of accomplishment that the seniors will have as they learn these pieces and are able to play them for others.

Think of the happiness that is associated with playing music, and then multiply that by making opportunities for seniors to showcase their skills. That could end up being in the form of small concerts throughout the week, or even concerts focused around season changes or holidays.

You might also consider doing talent shows, which leads us to another benefit of musical lessons. It sparks creativity, and your residents could end up writing songs

MUSICAL
RETIREMENT

and music of their own. Talent shows are a wonderful way for them to showcase their creativity. Plus, you can encourage residents to get together with each other, sparking more creative options in the form of duets or assemble pieces.

All of these additional activities can be a wonderful way to relax and provide good food for the souls of your residents. When you play an instrument, you are not only receiving the joy that comes from playing, but you are also going to pass that joy on to those who are listening to you.

It is Never Too Late

Some of your residents might be resistant to the idea of learning to play a musical instrument. After all, they might believe that they are too old to be learning something new. I want to make it clear that you are never too old to learn. There is no such thing as being unable to teach an old dog new tricks. Encourage your residents to open their minds to the idea of learning new ways to express themselves through music.

Playing music, particularly as you age, is an important part of staying healthy. No matter if they learn to play guitar, piano, accordion, or just about any instrument, the mind and muscle coordination is required to keep their brains active, and those benefits can spill over into other areas of their lives.

Notice that there are benefits, even if your residents are older and may not be able to play specific instruments due to size or weight. The old saying of a "body in motion tends to stay in motion" is true for your mind as well.

Learning or even continuing to grow in your expertise to play a musical instrument helps to keep your mind active can benefit a variety of areas in the lives of your residents.

There are also the therapeutic benefits of playing music. While your seniors might not have the same level of responsibilities that they once did, there is still a level of stress that is part of their lives. Playing music can be a relatively inexpensive escape that allows your residents to escape into the world of imagination and beauty, even it is just for a short period of time.

You can make connections with local businesses to provide lessons to residents. Our team also can assist in the process of helping your facility provide lessons or create a performance schedule for those individuals who are opting to learn an instrument.

If you are just starting a musical program for your residents, it can seem challenging to convince residents to give the idea a shot. However, once they get started, then their confidence and ability will grow. Before long, they will be amazed at what they are able to play and accomplish.

There is no age or point where you are too old to learn an instrument. Individuals have learned the guitar well into their 80s. Clearly, your residents do not have to be limited in their options.

Turning to Music During Challenging Periods

Once you learn an instrument, it can be a great way to deal with difficult challenges in your life. If you have residents dealing with unexpected medical diagnoses or the losses of family and friends, having the ability to play music can help them to cope.

Music can also be combined with visualization techniques to help them mentally handle the challenges that come with different diagnoses. Playing music can help your residents to sleep better, or they can even write lyrics to help them express their feelings. Composing new songs or music can help your residents feel connected to their future, especially during hard times.

That being said, encouraging creativity and playing musical instruments can be a way to reduce the stress and anxiety of your residents. Focusing on incorporating musical learning opportunities into your residents' daily routines can be a key opportunity to help them in multiple areas.

I also want to share that you do not have to limit musical learning opportunities to just learning an instrument. One option for your facility is building a choir. That means your residents bring the amazing instrument of their voices. Consider creating opportunities for your choir to showcase their talent and share their musical voices with the other residents.

Being able to sing in challenging circumstances is also a great way to help them manage their emotions and outlook, in a way that can bring positive benefits. Now let's talk about why being a good musician is amazing for your brain.

Being a Musician is Good for Your Brain

Science continues to prove the benefits of musical training. It can change brain structure and help your residents to function even better. The point of incorporating a musical retirement mentality involves finding ways to maximize the benefits of music for your residents. It means taking everyday activities and adding a musical twist.

For those residents that opt to take music lessons, then they also benefit from being musicians. As we age, the reality is that reaction times get slower. Playing a musical instrument can help your residents to increase their reaction times, giving them faster auditory, tactile, and audio-tactile reaction times. Musicians also are able to integrate lots of multisensory information in a way that others cannot.

Music does something unique, as it stimulates the brain in a very powerful way because of our emotional connections with music and the connections that it helps us to create. Unlike traditional brain games, playing an instrument provides a rich and complex experience, due to the fact that you are constantly integrating information from all of your senses. The result of continuing to play an instrument, or to sing, means that you are creating long-lasting changes in the brain.

Brain scanning studies find that anatomical changes are related to the age that they start learning an instrument. Clearly, there are greater benefits when you pick up an instrument at an earlier age, but there are also benefits even if you start later in life. Perhaps you have residents who played in the past; encourage them to pick that instrument back up or take their previous musical experience to another instrument.

After all, once you learn an instrument, the ability to read music or understand the various notes can be used to learn another instrument. Allow your residents to explore their interests, because you can be giving them positive benefits that will help them throughout the rest of the years of their lives.

Interestingly, even if they only have brief periods of musical training, they can still have the benefit of preserving sharp processing of speech sounds and increase their resilience to any age-related decline in hearing.

Here are a few other ways that musicians can benefit from their musical training, particularly if they are learning an instrument:

- Strengthens bonds with others

- Strengthens memory and reading skills

- Makes them happier by playing music

- Can process multiple things at once

- Helps the brain recover

- Reduces stress and depression

- Strengthens the brain's executive function

What is the executive function in your brain? It covers critical tasks, like processing and retaining information, controlling behavior, making decisions, and problem solving. Clearly, musical training can improve and strengthen executive functioning in adults, regardless of age.

As you can see, there are a variety of benefits that come from connecting with musical training and opportunities as a senior. I have shared a variety of ways that you might be able to incorporate music into your life or retirement facility. Now let's talk about how activity directors and facilities have enjoyed the experience of working with me and my team to bring music into their routine. May you be inspired to bring

MUSICAL
RETIREMENT

music into the lives of the seniors within your sphere of influence. For more information about these activities and other musical opportunities we offer, contact us at musicalretirement.com.

MUSICAL
RETIREMENT

CHAPTER 11

Experiences from Activity
Directors and Facilities

MUSICAL RETIREMENT

Here are some of the places that have been working with retirement homes, long-term facilities, nursing homes and different seniors' communities, our team has been inspired to keep providing these musical services to seniors in a variety of settings.

Here are a few examples from hundreds of retirement homes, long-term facilities, nursing homes and different senior communities Musical Retirement Corporation has been working with them.

Chartwell Retirement Residences has been working with the Musical Retirement Corporation. Staff and residents of their various residences have mentioned how much they enjoyed the musical activities led by our team.

Others mentioned how much they enjoyed working with me and our team because of the passion that we bring. At Chartwell Retirement Residences, our team focuses on bringing music to residents in different ways. "Ivgeni plays the saxophone beautifully but also has great character and personality to interact with our residents...He will walk around to each resident and guest, making them feel special and involved," said **Daniella Ventimiglia**, Lifestyle and Programs Manager.

The Program Manager from <u>Richview Manor</u>, said: "Ivgeni performs to reduce anxiety, improve mood, and make people happier. Ivgeni's music touches the lives of all who have the opportunity to listen, so we are all more than happy to welcome his remarkable talent and passion back to Richview."

E.B., Recreation Supervisor—<u>Belmont House</u>, wrote: "What we greatly appreciated was that Ivgeni moved throughout the room, allowing all residents to receive direct attention, and encouraging everyone to get involved. A very, very talented man; we are greatly appreciative that he shared his passion for helping others with us."

S.E., Director of Resident Program, <u>Muskoka Shores Care Community</u>, wrote: "Ivgeni is loved by all of our residents. His unique performance style engages all levels of seniors, which is exceptional and fun to watch. He has the ability to provide therapeutic music benefits while doing so in a lively and entertaining way."

Working with small and large companies that manage multiple facilities is enjoyable because our team is able to work with residents across their portfolio. Some facilities also offer an opportunity to bring unique musical services to their residents. Here are just a few of the experiences that we have enjoyed.

With <u>Revera Retirement Living or Long-Term Care</u>, we have been able to work with seniors in all stages of their retirement and long-term care. "Ivgeni knows how to play all the songs that seniors love to listen to on his saxophone. This is how he gets them engaged and dancing. Our residents enjoy being entertained, but sometimes they just want to sit and watch. Ivgeni's performance actually gets them standing up out of their chairs and involved in the entertainment. His energy and enthusiasm make the residents want to stand up and sing and dance. He has gotten residents to dance, who I have never seen dance before! The residents also enjoy dressing up in the accessories and costumes he brings. It is a great touch to his performance," said **M. C.**, Director of Recreation at one of the retirement homes by Revera. Ms. M.C. also noted that each of these activities got the seniors engaged and on their feet. "Ivgeni, being a Registered Nurse, knows the positive impact that music, dancing, and entertainment has on a senior's well-being and quality of life," she concluded.

"Besides playing the saxophone beautifully, what sets Ivgeni apart from most entertainers is his ability to engage with the residents during his performances. With Ivgeni, the residents don't just sit and listen; they are also a part of the performance. His ability to do this is even more impressive in our Special Care unit with residents whose cognition levels are quite low and exhibit responsive behaviors. The residents sing, dance, and laugh with him," said **M. F.**, Program Manager & Volunteer Coordinator for another home of Revera.

The Sienna Senior Living group of facilities has also been a wonderful place for the Musical Retirement team to share musical programs.

MUSICAL
RETIREMENT

"Our residents look forward to having Ivgeni here, and eagerly ask when he will be back after each visit. During his show, Ivgeni keeps all of the participants (including staff) engaged with music, lights, props, dancing, instruments, and his beautiful saxophone playing. He finds a way to get every resident involved, no matter what their capabilities may be. Everyone knows when he is in our building by the sound of music and laughter coming from our lobby," said **Tarah Belcourt**, Director of Resident Programs.

Other retirement facilities have continued to mention the importance of the interactions between our team and the residents in their facility. "Our community members raved about how talented he was, how diverse his songs were, and how fun the performance was," said **T. D.**, Lifestyles Manager of one of the <u>VIVA</u> retirement homes. At <u>VERVE Senior Living</u>, their team points to how medication is not enough to help people feel better or improve their quality of life. "With 20 years of hospital experience, Ivgeni's musical talents with the saxophone can be another layer to create benefits for our residents," said one of the activities managers at a VERVE Senior Living retirement home.

Working with community facilities, such as <u>Schlegel Villages</u>, gives our team a chance to interact with a wide variety of senior residents. The Schlegel Villages staff there told us about how much our programs have positively impacted their residents.

<u>The City of Toronto Long Term Homes</u> have been

working with our team regularly. "Ivgeni Kriger has been providing quality entertainment for our cognitively intact and impaired residents since last year. He is skilled in developing unique interactions with residents through his music, instruments, costumes, and props. Ivgeni is an interactive artist. He is able to evoke positive emotions and reactions that not all entertainers are able to do. He is passionate about his work, and works hard to reach residents from all walks of life," said **D. L.,** one of the managers of Resident Services at City of Toronto Long Term Homes.

Here are a few of the comments from individuals our team worked with that offered us the opportunity to work with seniors in several different locations within their facility systems.

"Ivgeni is a very friendly and pleasant person to talk to and coordinate what we expect from the performance. He was open to suggestions and willing to work hard to make sure the tenants had a great time. His talent went beyond just playing the saxophone, which he does amazingly, but his timing during the performance kept everyone engaged with anticipation for the next one," said **L. M.,** one of the Coordinators of Activation at Loft Community Services. "I think Ivgeni would make a great performer for almost any event, as his diversity shines through his saxophone and his passion for people."

"Ivgeni has been playing in our community for the last few years, and every time he performs, he enlightens

MUSICAL RETIREMENT

our residents' lives with his professionalism, passion, and charisma. Every time he plays in our community, he surprises us with something more dynamic, engaging, and interactive in his approach," said **Brayan Martinez**, the Life Enrichment Coordinator at <u>Tapestry Village Gate West</u>, part of Tapestry –The Art of Senior Living.

"It is with much pleasure that I acknowledge the remarkable entertaining program provided by Ivgeni Kriger to our senior population. I had the opportunity to celebrate Senior's Month by hiring Ivgeni to entertain three of my sites with his beautiful saxophone and interaction with the clients and residents that partook in the programs. My clientele incorporates my Supportive Housing and Life Lease sites that houses independent living, as well as my Adult Day Program that caters to seniors with dementia, all of whom thoroughly enjoyed his entertainment. Ivgeni provided a variety of props that all the clients and residents enjoyed partaking in, and interacted with the entire group, making them laugh, sing, clap, and interact with wonderful fellowship. My clients and residents have asked me to invite Ivgeni back again for future engagements, who has numerous theme-related occasions that will fit our desired event. A must-see entertainer to give pleasure to your senior population," said **M. H.**, Supervisor, Community Programs for the <u>County of Simcoe</u>—Long Term Care and Seniors Services.

"I have hired Ivgeni on multiple occasions as a solo saxophone entertainer within Long Term Care, as well as retirement communities in the Toronto area. I continue to have him return because he brings a lifetime of experience to what he does, but also because the residents adore his big personality and exceptional talent when it comes to playing the saxophone. Ivgeni Kriger has the ability to turn a dull afternoon into a lively music filled one, where the staff even walk by to determine where all of the laughter, clapping, and singing or playing along comes from. He gets residents up off of their seats to dance along, play instruments, or engage by having them dress up for the occasion. It is incredible to watch him quickly transform the room so that by the end of the hour, residents are hand in hand, singing along to their all-time favorite songs they grew up with…My residents have always requested his return and thoroughly look forward to his performance, as he is an exceptional musician but also a wonderful person as a whole," said one of the Life Enrichment Coordinators for the ΛMICA Senior Lifestyles system.

"As the Manager of Recreation and Volunteer Services at <u>Villa Leonardo Gambin Long Term Care Home</u>, I highly recommend Mr. Ivgeni Kriger's interactive musical performance services. We have been inviting Mr. Kriger into our home on a monthly basis for almost a year now, and we are extremely satisfied with the services he provides. Mr. Kriger is professional, creative, and passionate about his work; he actively engages residents regardless of age, gender, ethnicity, or physical and cognitive limitations. Equipped with a nursing background, Mr. Kriger is able to safely work independently and does not require immediate supervision or assistance with his program. He is efficient in setting up, gathering residents, facilitating the program, and tidying up afterwards, leaving staff free to facilitate other programs at the same time. Mr. Kriger offers a unique and interactive musical program, which provides residents with stimulation, socialization, feelings of belonging and acceptance, and general happiness. Mr. Kriger's program is different each time it is facilitated as it is tailored to the residents that are present and to the time of year, upcoming holidays, etc....We will continue to invite Mr. Kriger into our home as we strongly believe that his program has a significant impact on the quality of life of our residents," said **Louise Facca**, Manager of Recreation and Volunteer Services of <u>Villa Leonardo Gambin</u>.

"Ivgeni is one of the most interactive showmen I personally have ever witnessed in senior living entertainment. His involvement includes props to create atmosphere, items for the residents to use to keep the beat and to clap along to, and as for himself, he has costumes to invoke the theme of the afternoon. Ivgeni's saxophone playing creates a truly sing-along fun day for our seniors. Ivgeni has many styles and music types that he uses in different senior living residences, for all cultures to enjoy. His entire show, as he tells me, is simply to make people happy and enjoy all kinds of music, as music is an international language that many people love," said **Don Lemieux**, Executive Director of the <u>Weston Gardens Retirement Residences</u>.

One of the parts of growing my team and business over the years is reaching back to facilities and their personnel for feedback on their experience with our classes and seminars. As I review the feedback, the one constant is how much of an impact our classes and activities have on the seniors who participate.

Another positive that various facilities have found is the fact that my team can judge and access the residents' abilities, thus creating an experience that leaves them feeling built up, instead of frustrated because of all the areas where they couldn't participate.

"Ivgeni saw what residents could do, and he used props, musical instruments, and recorded and live music and dance to involve residents in his program. He encouraged residents to sing and move their arms while sitting in their wheelchairs, to play an instrument and, if ambulatory, to dance. He even danced with residents in their wheelchairs," said **L. J.**, the program manager at one of <u>Revera's</u> long-term homes.

Overall, time and again, the various managers that I have come in contact with talk about how our team has worked with the residents and created a fun, engaging experience. Perhaps you are looking to create a similar experience with your residents.

Our team can talk with you about the activities we offer to facilities, as well as the various senior-based seminars that give your residents the ability to enjoy

MUSICAL
RETIREMENT

music in all areas of their lives. It builds them up and spreads joy.

"The first time I met Ivgeni, he told me that his goal was to make a million seniors happy. He has definitely made an impact towards that goal at Spencer House. The smiles he puts on the faces of our residents last long after he is gone," said **Tarah Belcourt**, Director of Resident Programs at <u>Spencer House Care Community</u>. Another aspect of the experience that we bring to facilities is that we can take musical activities to the next level.

"We are fortunate to have many talented entertainers perform at our facility and provide entertainment to our residents. Ivgeni has raised the bar for "musiking" to a whole new level. Ivgeni actually walks about to all the residents and engages them to some level of their ability," said **Aurika Bennett**, activity manager at <u>Salvation Army Eventide Home</u>.

We see the benefits of bringing social opportunities to seniors, many of whom are content to stay in their rooms by themselves. We also create a diverse experience for you, your love ones or your residents, tapping into their musical tastes and history.

Truly, music has the power to make a difference in the lives of seniors, regardless of their cognitive or physical abilities. Please contact us at musicalretirement. com today to learn more about how we can help you to incorporate music into the lives of your senior family members, yourself or those who are part of your facility!

MUS|CAL
RET|REMENT

CHAPTER 12

Engaging with Seniors—
Musical Activities

MUSICAL RETIREMENT

Throughout this book, I have shared a variety of musical activities that my team offers in our and your facility, and the ones that we have shared with seniors and retirement facilities. Now, I want to share what some of the various facilities we work with view as key activities and methods to improve the overall quality of their residents' lives.

See what others think about these types of musical activities, and if you are interested in incorporating some of our musical activities and seminars, then please contact our team today through musicalretirement.com! "Music is a Segway to conversation and connection of the past, present, and the future. Music is an avenue of communication with those affected by dementia and Alzheimer's, as well as others with cognitive decline… we use music to calm residents, to trigger memory, and to connect people with their culture, as well as with their faith. We use music at bath time, bedtime, and at the end of life. Music has been an important part of the human existence across the world since the existence of time," said **Major Renée Clarke**, director of spiritual care at <u>Eventide Nursing Home</u> in Niagara Falls, who also serves as that facility's chaplain. "Rhythm was the first sound we all heard when we were conceived in our mother's womb. Her heartbeat and our own was the first metronome of our lives and we are born with it. Because long-term memories are the last to leave in the process of dementia and end of life, music is also one of the last communication pathways that reach the soul."

Major Clarke also noted how music can be a companion, offering a compassionate, non-invasive, non-threatening, and non-verbal means of self-expression and communication at the end of life care. "Music, so powerfully affecting our emotions and our memories, is also a central means of experiencing and expressing the sacred. Touch, eye contact, and interaction is also very important because it validates presence and connection." "I firmly believe that recreation can be more beneficial than medication in many situations. Life is about enjoyment at any age. Smile more, laugh more, and live as fully as you can. A lot of music helps too!" — **Ashley MacGregor**, Activity Coordinator at <u>Birchmere Retirement Residence</u>.

"I think the most important thing for team members, when working with senior residents, is to get to know the resident as best they can—their likes, dislikes, history, routines, preferences, passions, and family dynamics. Understanding what motivates the resident and using that to create a care plan, and sharing the information with all team members, is of the utmost importance."—**Debbie McCance**, Activity Director at <u>Chartwell Gibson</u>.

"A background where music is played softly in the background eases the palate and sets the pace for mealtime. Music is an added ingredient that you will not find in any cookbook. If you are having an Italian Night, play some Italian music; a Scottish Night, play Scottish music—all the ingredients for an enjoyable mealtime."— **Roger Dee**, Lifestyle and Program Manager at <u>Chartwell Parkway</u>, with over 30 years' experience working with seniors, both in retirement and long-term care.

"Here at our home, we believe that daily morning exercise is the best activity a senior can do daily. We have classes that run every morning…these exercises are done both standing and sitting, and involve the use of weights and stretching bands. For those seniors who cannot or do not like to participate in group exercise, they are offered a walk outside or in the building with a staff member for some one-on-one time and friendly conversation…I found out a few weeks back that one of the residents here on our Memory Care Floor, who suffers from dementia, used to bake every weekend up at her cottage. So, I took her to the kitchen early this morning and helped her bake peanut butter and chocolate chip cookies. Afterwards, she asked if she could wash the dishes, and then proceeded to wash down the counter tops and clean the floor as if she was in her own home. Not only did she laugh and smile the entire time while she reminisced about her past, but this resident continued to talk about her morning and baking for the remainder of the day. In turn, she became more social with others living in the home. Seniors and health care workers more often than not form close

MUSICAL RETIREMENT

bonds and friendships. I would say the most important role for staff in health care is to fulfill every aspect of a senior's life, which is emotionally, physically, mentally, and spiritually." — **Danielle Wright**, Activity Director at Georgian Bay Seniors Lodge.

"I don't think there is particularly one important activity. I think it is a balance of the following: cognitive, physical, and spiritual well-being. I find that everyone performs at their best when all these needs are met. However, everyone is different. Some people are fueled more through physical or social activity. It is important to recognize your clientele and shape your scope of services around their interests. I think the most important activity that staff can offer to improve the lives of their clients is by offering new and exciting experiences. I find it is difficult to bring people out of their comfort zones; however, with a little trial and error, you can discover what works best." — **Yalda Hoshmand**, Activity Director at North York Seniors Centre.

"It's by making sure we enable/facilitate the hope for a better tomorrow by working on and through the seven dimensions of wellness (physical, emotional, intellectual, social, spiritual, environmental, and occupational). It is important to engage the seniors in all the different dimensions, in order to achieve an active lifestyle, which will decrease the challenges they go through every day and will increase the opportunities of having a better charge of their health and wellness.

Having proper training and understanding of the

environment that you are working at is very important for you to be able to achieve the senior's expectations and needs. Working for seniors is a very fulfilling experience, and it requires a lot of passion and love in order to achieve the seven dimensions of wellness."— **Brayan Martinez**, Activity Director at <u>Tapestry</u>.

"I believe that participating in meaningful activities and having meaningful interactions with others is one of the most important things in a person's day. As we get older, we tend to withdraw from previously enjoyed activities, such as hobbies and social events, which can lead to social isolation and depression. In my experience, seniors can sometimes feel that they no longer serve a purpose or contribute to society, and that can play a big role in their self-worth and quality of life. Finding ways to empower seniors by making them feel wanted, needed, and accepted can have a tremendous impact on their quality of life. Providing seniors with opportunities to socialize, be themselves, and feel like they have a purpose is one of the most important ways we can empower seniors and improve their quality of life."—**Louise Facca**, BSc. Recreation, CTRS. Manager of Recreation and Volunteer Services at <u>Villa Leonardo Gambin</u>.

"The most important thing in senior living is social interaction. Often, when seniors move into retirement, they revert to isolation, resulting in a decline in mood. Low energy and low mood levels often contribute to dementia symptoms. Entertainment is a great way to improve quality of life as residents have a chance to socially engage with one another as well as engage with the musician. It is also a chance to benefit from music therapy…the staff must do all they can to promote the importance of social interaction."—**Riley Braj**, Life Enrichment Manager at <u>Verve Senior Living</u>.

"The most important activity in a senior's daily life is interaction. Seniors do so much better mentally and physically when they interact with others; even if it is simply a hello or a handshake, they feel valued and worthwhile if they connect with even one person. The most important activity that someone working with seniors can do is listen. It may be regarding a health issue or might be an upset or frustration, or just to have their voice heard. It is very important for workers to take the time to listen to what is being said, in order to make the resident feel validated and respected. Sometimes all that a resident wants is to talk, and other times it can lead to a problem being solved or an issue being brought to light. For some, it provides an opportunity to share their story or re-live their best memories."— **Becky MacDonald**, Activity Coordinator, <u>Granite Ridge Retirement Residence</u>.

"Getting to know a resident's past and present will help to establish and work towards a better future for them. Providing quality programs and care is critical and important; however, in order for us to do that, we need to get to know our residents on many levels. Activities can range from various things, such as physical, social, emotional, spiritual, and vocal. That is why it is important to understand an individual before creating programs and inviting them to programs. Music plays a huge role in making a true impact on our residents. I believe that no matter what your culture is and where you are from, music brings everyone together on both a social and emotional level."—**Elizabeth Minichillo**, Activity Director at <u>Chartwell Pine Grove Long Term</u>.

In the end, surveying these people who have such a critical role in the lives of seniors helped me to understand that listening and maintaining as much independence as possible is the key to helping seniors have a better quality of life, regardless of where they are physically or mentally.

If you are trying to figure out the next level of activities, or how to move your facility in a new direction, then contact our team today to learn more about what we can offer to you, your loved ones and your seniors!

Remember that musicalretirement.com wants to help every senior to feel happier!

MUSICAL
RETIREMENT

About the Author

Ivgeni Kriger is an Author, Registered Nurse, Entrepreneur, Professional Musician, Lawyer and owner of the Musical Retirement Corporation. Throughout his time working in the nursing field, Ivgeni noted how music could serve to lift the moods of those who were in his care. That led to him moving out of the nursing field and exploring how music could be incorporated into all areas of senior care. The idea behind Musical Retirement was born. Today, Ivgeni works with various retirement homes, long-term facilities, nursing homes and different seniors' communities to incorporate musical activities and events throughout their routine. No matter the size of the facility or operations, Ivgeni and his wonderful staff can provide a variety of musical options including outdoor parties.

Today, Ivgeni Kriger continues to expand his offerings for seniors around the world and to establish the first in the world, Musical Retirement Homes.

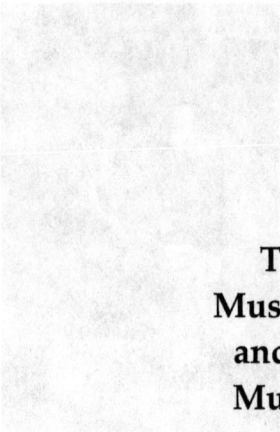

To learn more about
Musical Retirement Home
and Ivgeni Kriger, go to
MusicalRetirement.com